THE
TEN TENETS
of
BUSINESS SUCCESS

ROSEMARY HARRIS-LOXLEY

PREFACE

Who am I writing for?

I am writing for entrepreneurs, executives of small and medium-sized enterprises (SMEs) who are interested in business growth, managers keen to improve their business performance, and supporters of entrepreneurship.

Structure and content

This book examines the recognizable features and traits of entrepreneurial thinking and then follows with chapters on each of ten tenets (or principles) inherent in business effectiveness. These should provide the entrepreneur with an easy-to-read set of guidelines for ongoing success.

What is different?

This book is written from a basis of over twenty years' personal experience of coaching directors of small and medium-sized enterprises, many of whom started their businesses from scratch or inherited family businesses and were determined to make them grow and change. This is not a report of findings from an academic study of entrepreneurs, but observations based on the characteristics those people displayed and their responses to facilitation of their personal development. If I had written this book earlier, it would have been the handbook supplied in the "Business Performance Workshop" program which was the starting point of the long and fruitful relationships between myself and the personalities involved, many of whom are now in the category of lifelong friends.

Style

This is a non-academic and practical book which addresses the reader from a personal perspective. It contains a number of questionnaires for those who may want to analyze their own situations, but completion is not strictly necessary. Often, just reading some of the questions is sufficient to set off a chain of thoughts in the entrepreneurial mind that triggers a significant set of actions. Entrepreneurs tend to be creatures who prefer to act rather than study, and this book can be picked up and opened at any chapter. The chapters are short, by design, and each one carries its own message so it can be read and used in isolation from the others.

THE CONTENTS

The introduction explains the importance of self-awareness and personal effectiveness to anyone with aspirations of business success. It contains a questionnaire for personal analysis, taking into consideration the inevitable impact of work satisfaction and effectiveness on personal life and vice versa. It also lists the ten tenets of business success.

Chapter 1 discusses the phenomenon of the many businesspeople who cannot express, or have forgotten, their original *raison d'être* and how that has damaged them. This chapter advocates the importance of recognizing the difference between *why they are in business* and *how they will conduct their business*. It also explores the benefits of common understanding of the priorities when the organization is impacted by a variety of influences, both internal and external. This chapter highlights the benefits of a well-balanced team of *decision thinkers* at a decision-making level and how this can be achieved.

This chapter is based on the assertion that the true purpose of any manager can be described in only four words: to achieve desired results. This applies at any level and in any kind of business in the world. Within that purpose lies the responsibility to obtain an appropriate return on the investment of the resources utilized in the business.

Fifteen key areas of resources are listed, and the chapter examines how performance and contribution can be ascertained and monitored. Emphasis is placed upon the benefits of team awareness and shared accountability.

There is an acknowledgement that the ultimate accountability for management of all resources lies with the leader, so the successful entrepreneur learns how to keep informed whilst delegating. This is particularly important to those individuals who have started their businesses from personal resources and may be reluctant to let go because of risks involved.

Chapter 3   **Tenet No. 3—Focus on Critical Success Factors**

Chapter 3 suggests a simple-to-use methodology for enabling the leader of the business to monitor the performance of all aspects of the business with up-to-date information. It follows on from the assertion in the previous chapter, highlighting the need for mutual understanding of current priorities and agreed reporting practices between the leader and those with delegated responsibilities.

Chapter 4   **Tenet No. 4—Accountability for Contribution**

This chapter comments on the relative merits of various organizational cultures, with particular reference to the nature of accountability, based on management of relationships. This is discussed with observations of the responses to management communication in examples of small companies headed by classic entrepreneurial types, as opposed to large institutionalized organizations. It also explores the value of introducing appraisal systems into small operational units and the subsequent effect of alternative approaches.

Chapter 5   **Tenet No. 5—Optimum Risk Management**

This chapter explores implications of risk taking within the context of investment, cultural norms, differing attitudes, availability of relevant information, costs, and benefits to the business.

It also returns to the theme of a whole-brain approach to team problem solving and decision making.

Chapter 6   **Tenet No. 6—Shared Values**

Chapter 6 explains the "stakeholder" philosophy of a company headed by a visionary leader, able to stimulate a sense of participation in the creation of the company's own success model.

It also explores whether *charisma* is a necessary ingredient for achieving outstanding leadership success or not, within the context of differing styles of leadership and differing cultural expectations.

Chapter 7   **Tenet No. 7—Morale Maintenance**

This chapter is concerned with the energizing elements influencing the culture within a working unit. Comparisons are drawn between various examples of prevailing organizational cultures, based on the apparent values and norms displayed.

There is a brief explanation of the "life script" concept from Eric Berne's theory of *transactional analysis* which, it is suggested, affects the expectations and responses of people regarding working relationships.

Chapter 8   **Tenet No. 8—Culture of Participation**

Chapter 8 follows on from the previous chapter and introduces the cycle of actions leading to orientation of working groups towards desired results achievement. It deals with the importance of communication and issues of integrity and with the dilemmas which a truly participative approach can present, particularly to an entrepreneur who has originated the business from small beginnings. This chapter highlights the importance of objectivity and prioritizing that which is best for the business as opposed to personal loyalties and long-term relationships.

Chapter 9   **Tenet No. 9—Monitoring Elements of Impact**

This chapter refers to the assertion that good managers "know what's going on" and deals with the importance of being alert to developments outside the business, as well as inside, that can significantly affect its performance, stability, or operation.

It also highlights the benefits of observing trends and considering potential implications with a view to dealing with exigencies in ways which minimize negative impact, or alternatively present new opportunities.

This chapter questions assumptions made about growth as a criterion for measuring success in business and deals with issues of the effect of changes inherent in business growth, together with implications for leadership and systems of operating.

Chapter 10   **Tenet No. 10—Continuous Learning Environment**

Chapter 10 advocates a commitment to fostering opportunities for learning at every level of a company. This entails the recognition of how people learn as well as the benefits of mentorship, coaching, tolerance of mistakes, and sharing of knowledge.

It also explains the need for avoidance of "blame culture" and for encouragement of self-managed personal development, identification of transferable skills, and whole-brain thinking.

Chapter 11 Summary—The Pre-eminent Role of Thinking in Entrepreneurship

This chapter reiterates the significance of high awareness of various thinking styles and how each of these is particularly beneficial, and should be utilized, for different aspects of business operation.

It asserts that professional thinking is the prime function of the leader and top team in a growing business, and, as such, is a key area for personal development for executives.

This chapter suggests that entrepreneurship will be severely limited, in the context of aspiration, without attention to increasing overall thinking capabilities.

It also recommends activities for development of thinking skills.

Readership

This book is mainly aimed at entrepreneurs themselves who may have been in business for some time. It will also appeal to new starters who are serious about growth as opposed to limiting their operation.

Because of its emphasis on the relevance of thinking styles, including the references to cultural traits, it would be of interest to trainers and coaches of entrepreneurs in any country.

The fact that this book is based on personal experience of the author's work in helping owners of businesses in the small and medium-sized category for many years also makes it a useful read in business schools. Also, the author's background in training provides credibility to those chapters dealing with aspects of people management.

BIOGRAPHICAL DETAILS

ROSEMARY HARRIS-LOXLEY

Based in Lincolnshire, Rosemary is a Business Performance Improvement Coach, with over twenty-five years' experience, working with companies of all sizes and sectors of industry, ranging from multinationals to medium-sized enterprises.

Specializing in the implications of business development and change, she uses innovative approaches, including *Brain Mapping*, to help executives identify their personal thinking style and the inherent implications relating to particular job roles. This facilitates improved organizational application of particular strengths and a general widening of thinking and communication ability within working groups. The objective is to enhance team participation and leadership skills through increased awareness of the significant differences in contribution that individuals can and do make to successful businesses.

She has implemented business growth projects that have totally changed the performance of various companies by close involvement at every level of the business, including personal coaching of managing directors and executive teams. This coaching was supplemented by an in-house training program specially designed and delivered to managers and staff.

Rosemary holds fellowships of the RSA and the Chartered Institute of Personnel Development as well as membership of the Institute of Management and the Institute of Sales and Marketing Management, from whom she has been awarded a gold medal for excellence.

She has been an assessor as well as a regional judge for the National Training Award and a director of the commercial arm of The Centre for Tomorrow's Company.

Seven years with the Distributive Industry Training Board gave Rosemary a strong background in the skills of facilitating learning activities of others at every level of business. This, coupled with her proven record of coaching business leaders to create their own success, means that all of her work is derived from personal recommendations of clients who respect the contribution she has made to their business growth as executives and leaders.

PREVIOUS PUBLICATIONS:

Rosemary coauthored a chapter on small and medium-sized firms in a book entitled *Management Consultancy*, edited by Philip Sadler and published by Kogan Page.

She self-published a guide to retail selling (as a training aid), entitled *The Retail Sales Consultant*. It was produced originally as a supplement to a culture change program being delivered prior to the launch of the "next" retail multiple chain and was used in every branch. This was later purchased by other retail chains and was also customized on behalf of the Thomas Cook travel organization.

ACKNOWLEDGEMENTS

This book might not have been completed without the great encouragement I received, at various stages, from some young people who surprised me by the level of enthusiasm they displayed after reading the early chapters. Although they are members of my family, they are all intelligent, successful people whose judgment I respect. Samantha Loxley, Helen Brooks, Christopher Brooks, and Andrew Irwin each urged me to believe that my project was worthwhile, even when I was convinced that it would have limited appeal in the marketplace.

The book is meant to guide an entrepreneur through the challenging pathways of business growth and development. The reader will notice the difference in the style and terminology of the later chapters as I envisaged my entrepreneur engaged in the process of managing the growth of a relatively small business to one that would become, or already was becoming, something much larger.

This shift in style and emphasis was noted by Kevin James when he, too, took the trouble to read the first draft. As a senior executive in a multinational automobile manufacturing company, he was quick to question the change.

The book is an attempt to encapsulate many of the learning points that arose during the running of action-learning workshops and their supportive coaching element that I designed and led together with a very creative colleague and friend, Terry Cook. These also involved input from a brilliant financial management coach, Vivian Stokes (see Chapter 9). Between us, during the lifetime of the "Business Performance Workshop" series, we helped to turn at least 150 directors representing a large variety of small organizations into strategic business operators who were excited about the future and what could be achieved. Those men and women, many of whom I now count amongst my very best friends, also deserve my gratitude for proving the truth of my belief in the potential of human beings when they are motivated and determined to keep learning from their experiences and mistakes along the way. My life has been enriched by their successes, and this book is dedicated to them.

Last but by no means least, I have to thank my husband Gerry Loxley for patiently listening when I needed to read some chapters aloud to him so that I could hear if my words were making sense. His own experience as a senior executive of a manufacturing company sometimes prompted him to ask some very practical questions that made me reconsider the way I was expressing my thoughts.

One thing though is certain. The person who has been my driving force in getting this book to publication stage is the previously mentioned Andrew Irwin whose career as an officer in the U.S. Army contributed a sense of commitment to the concept of finishing what you start!

There have also been three stalwarts who have helped me at moments of stress when I have struggled with computer rage when attempting to submit illustrations. Thank you my dear friends: Rosemary Broom, Jon Crook, Nicky Stephen.

THE TEN TENETS OF BUSINESS SUCCESS

The Reason for Writing this Book

There are many reasons for writing a book, just as there are many books on the subject of business. So why is this book being written? Quite simply, in the thirty years that I have spent helping people to improve their skills in all kinds of business operations, there have emerged a number of fundamentals that prove that, in spite of all the innovations, global technology, and fads that come and go, some things never change.

There is also the fact that, throughout that time, I have been helped and motivated by reading hundreds of books by others. Those which have sparked a train of thought which has taken me down a new pathway or helped me to find an answer that had been eluding me have been most rewarding.

Many of my friends, colleagues, and participants of my training programs have been asking me for years why I have not yet written a book of my own. The answer is that it has been in my "good intentions box" for a long time. That box is the one I describe to others as having a very heavy lid, and the key keeps getting lost so that the stuff in it rarely comes out again. Too many of our wonderful plans and resolutions go into the box, and we never quite find the time to turn them into reality.

At last then, I am attempting to put down, in an easy-to-read form, the summary of principles of effectiveness in business whether you, dear reader, are a leader, a beginner, a trainer, or just somebody who wants to generally get it right in order to enjoy your work. Most of all, however, this book is aimed at those interested in entrepreneurship, whether they are one of that splendid breed or one of those who believe that entrepreneurs should be recognized, appreciated, and encouraged.

The title indicates my belief in the unchanging nature of basic principles about people, making things work, and the importance of results for effort. Too often, though, the results are never as spectacular as they could have been because we "kill off" the geese that can lay the golden eggs purely by neglecting them and failing to nurture them.

CONTENTS

Page

DEFINITION OF A TENET:

Principle, dogma, doctrine of a person or school

Ref. The Concise Oxford Dictionary

a.   1619. (he) holds, 3rd person singular of *tenere* hold; superceded earlier TENENT.

A doctrine, dogma, principle or opinion, in religion, philosophy, politics, or the like held by a school, sect, party or person.

b.   1630. Generally any opinion held.

The general tenet of all philosophers 1619
The master of Benet is of the like tenet GRAY 1630

Ref. The Shorter Oxford English Dictionary, Third Edition Reprinted 1988

INTRODUCTION

The Philosophy of the Ten Tenets

It is probably a coincidence that the number ten has cropped up in this little book of golden rules for business effectiveness in that it has a parallel with the Ten Commandments. I do not mind that as it is intended to serve a similar purpose as a checklist for living. Living at work, that is. There is no doubt that the rules we have decided to accept instinctively guide our decisions about how we should do things on a day-to-day basis. Most of us are pretty clear about those things the Ten Commandments dictate, so even when we flout them we are aware of the potential risk involved. I would like you to regard the ten tenets in the same way.

Their headings are:

- Clarity of purpose
- Knowledge and best use of resources
- Focus on critical success factors
- Accountability for contribution
- Optimum risk management
- Shared values
- Morale maintenance
- Culture of participation
- Monitoring elements of impact
- Continuous learning environment

Each of these will be explored from three viewpoints because they can affect us in various ways. For example:

(a)   The effect on ourselves on a personal level
(b)   The effect on our colleagues
(c)   The implications within the culture or society of which we are part

We all know that there are no magic wands in life, so this book is not offering instant panacea answers to the issues being explored, but what it will do is encourage you to become your own analyst. Although most problems are experienced by all of us at some time or other, the implications within the various options for dealing with them are never wholly the same. We each have our own cocktail of obstacles, both real and imaginary, as well as our own unique set of strengths and resources. If you are running, or are planning to run, a business enterprise, you are probably recognizing the need to make some changes, or you would not be reading this book. The alternative to making changes is to leave things as they are, so why would you be interested in business success if you are already satisfactorily successful? Is it because you feel that there are some untapped strengths or resources that could be more productive if some aspects were to be changed?

In organizations however large or small, making changes invariably has implications that are not always fully considered. This can frequently result in painful consequences that could have been avoided, or at least lessened, had the right kind of forethought taken place and the appropriate questions been asked. There can be a need to stimulate wider consideration of the effects of possible outcomes or the impact upon those affected.

This is why you will find checklists and questionnaires referred to in a number of chapters. You can then choose how you will deal with issues emerging from your responses. You may even decide to produce simple schedules for initiating the things you intend to do, but remember, only take the time to do this if you are really committing yourself.

Do not waste your time and energy producing action plans that might only end up in the dreaded box with the lost key—*The Good Intentions Box*!

In order to get you started, the first questionnaire—sometimes ruefully referred to as "Rosemary's Torture Document"—will help to clarify those things, on a very personal level, which will provide you with that clarity of purpose which is the subject of the first of the ten tenets.

In his book *The 4%*, written in 1984, Dr. Gerald Kushel describes people who enjoy total success in both their business and personal lives as Fully Effective Executives (FEEs). The main thrust of his book is that FEEs come in all shapes, sizes, and ages, from all racial and religious groups, and are of both sexes. Kushel also observes that these people always take full responsibility for their own actions and behavior, and I believe that therein lies one mark of the truly adult person. That observation coincides with the philosophy behind the questionnaire located at the end of this book that I have titled, rather challengingly:

What Am I Doing Here Anyway?

There are some crucial moments in life for many of us when we ask ourselves this very question, or one very like it. WAIDHA, as it has become known, is based on my firm belief that you cannot wholly separate the effect of work on your personal life, and similarly you cannot ignore the impact of your personal life on your ongoing performance in your job, whatever it is. Sometimes, of course, one of these can compensate for the other when all is not well, but if we aspire to be fully effective executives in Kushel's terms, we have to be honest with ourselves. This means that we should take stock of our situation and decide what we can do to make, or influence, the changes that would make the difference.

WAIDHA concentrates on the job dimension, but it does not preclude you from taking the personal things into consideration, particularly when considering your "support system" as one of your resources for helping your career or business development. The questionnaire has been designed to help you to analyze your role and function within your own organization and to identify any areas in which you may feel some action or change is necessary.

If you prefer to examine areas for change specifically in your personal life, the second document may be more helpful to you. I have entitled it: **My New Beginning—A Personal Contract**. It is at the end of this book after WAIDHA questionnaire. This is particularly appropriate if you have a sense of uneasiness or frustration about any aspect of your life. There are times when you need to examine how much of your time and energy is actually being spent in activities that make a real contribution towards turning your aspirations into realities.

We can easily slip into spending too much of our time doing things that benefit others at the expense of our own needs, or we habitually indulge in non-productive activities because they are easier or more enjoyable than the stuff that would take us more rapidly towards those aspirations. It is often all too easy to think, *I'll really make a start on that this week (or tomorrow)*. The trouble is, suddenly tomorrow has become yesterday, and that "start" has gone into our good intentions box. This is why it must become a personal contract with yourself that you regard as just as binding as any that you would sign when committing yourself to another person or organization. The commitment (or obligation) must be equally serious—it is a contract after all!

When completing either of these change documents, it is important that you answer as factually and truthfully as you can in order that it really fulfills its purpose. After all, you are not doing this to impress anyone; you are doing it to take charge of your own destiny. Sometimes the constraints we perceive are real, but in some instances they are the product of our own fears, insecurities, or simply our failure to address them. This is an excellent opportunity for you to examine developments within your own sphere of responsibility and to make some constructive comments (addressed to yourself) leading towards some positive decisions taken from a base of objectivity.

Each questionnaire is a private and personal analysis document that you may choose to complete as such, or you may wish to concentrate only on certain questions that stimulate a more in-depth examination of specific areas of relevance.

Some people find the WAIDHA document a useful basis for discussion with colleagues in order to clarify their full understanding of each of the questions or to enhance the expansion of their thoughts on each topic. Others prefer to deal with the analysis on a completely private and quiet basis. The choice is yours. However, it is advisable to view the WAIDHA analysis as a starting point and to refer back to it periodically to monitor your own progress. Upon completion, what you should have identified are those significant things which you can convert into goals. These can be the means of getting the focus that is so crucial to achievement of personal success.

There is an interesting little hierarchy which you can use when your goals are very challenging. Differentiate between your *Goals,* your *Aims*, and your *Objectives.*

Your **Goals**   are your desired results—the things you really want to achieve.

Your **Aims**   are those things over which you do not have full control but must influence because they contribute to, or affect, your outcomes.

Your **Objectives** are the things you can and will initiate and follow through because you know you can if you have the will and determination. In other words, they are SMART. Many of you will have heard of this before, but for those who have not, here is the explanation.

SMART is an acronym which serves as an *aide-memoire* for clarifying the rules about objectives. In order to be an objective, your chosen step must be:
Specific   *something definite you can identify*
Measurable   *set criteria for charting progress*
Achievable   *within your personal control*
Realistic   *even if stretching, it is attainable*
Time-bound   *within a foreseeable timeframe*

Remember—making your objectives achievable and realistic will ensure that you are not setting yourself up for failure, and making them specific, measurable, and time-bound will enable you to see yourself getting there. Then you can celebrate your progress and feel encouraged to keep up the effort.

You will find the questionnaires in the final part of this book. They can be used individually or as a pair because they complement each other. They both are designed to make you think hard about your priorities in terms of improving your current situation and to reach decisions about what you will do in the very near future. You should remember, of course, that in order to satisfactorily implement radical changes in an organization, you should have a strategy. This is especially important if you want to be perceived as a good manager or leader during the change process. If your people are to retain confidence in your ability to envisage and achieve a better state than that which existed before profound changes were initiated, they must instinctively feel that any action taken has been well considered and will eventually produce a good end result.

The first tenet has particular relevance to those who lead or hope to influence others. In the following chapter, you will find the transcript of a talk called "Strategy for Change" that I once delivered a number of years ago on the subject of change. My feelings about it have changed very little in the light of continued observations of managers I subsequently came across in a very wide assortment of organizations.

CHAPTER 1

Tenet Number 1—Clarity of Purpose

"Companies survive and prosper by being better than competitors at providing what people want or need."

Effective Marketing, by Geoffrey Randall

It is quite surprising how many people in business find it difficult to articulate the purpose of their business. When asked, they sometimes say, "Oh yes, we have a mission statement," and occasionally they can even tell you what that is! At this stage, it is often very apparent that they are unclear about the difference between *why they are in business* and *how they will conduct their business*. If they could take themselves back to their beginnings, they would probably realize that their business was started to fulfill a particular need at the time (one of the fundamentals of marketing). They became successful and stayed that way whilst they were concentrating on what they were good at, but when growth became their purpose, their focus became blurred. This is one key reason why so many organizations, having expanded into many different sectors in their eagerness to grow, one day realized their mistake and decided to go back to their "core business" as a means of recovering from serious downward trends in their performance and results. They had forgotten what they were in business for in the first place.

The leaders of those organizations had chosen to forget the original *raison d'être* of their companies, so the people who served them were no longer able to identify with either their product or their ethos. Without that identification, the likelihood is that the people had ceased to feel the sense of commitment and loyalty that derives from pride in the entity of which one is a part. Companies who have maintained a clear focus on *what they bring to the marketplace, and why*, invariably have a record of long-term success. Their leaders are very explicit about their continuing purpose and the future direction. When this is made apparent, it enables managers to clarify individual contribution towards the fulfillment of the company's purpose. Those who are part of the organization can then say, "This is why we are in business; this is where we are going, and this is what I contribute."

When we know the purpose of the business, it is easier to identify the purpose of our job and thereby our own purpose within it. If it is perceived, as it often is, that the purpose is merely to make money, the emotional energy of the organization gradually diminishes. The evidence of this lies in the large number of examples of highly successful organizations coming to grief because of decisions made, in pursuit of short-term profits, which have resulted in irrecoverable losses of other valuable resources. Their original purpose was subsumed to a subordinate position in their priorities, and the subsequent effect proved to be disastrous.

When values associated with loyalty to customers, staff, suppliers, and the wider community are apparently sacrificed, the major risk is that the people involved will take their loyalties, expertise, and energies elsewhere. These are resources that are very costly to replace.

A most important asset that organizations can have—and the one which too many inwardly focused heads of businesses started to disregard during the heady years of cost reduction, rationalization, and productivity improvement—is their customer base. With so many of Britain's companies led by accountants, the love affair with numbers that was encouraged by the "short-termism" of the stock market and the banking industry eventually caused the erosion in market share which they should have foreseen. This lack of appreciation of the value of relationships and mutual interests resulted in the loss of market share to competitors.

Unfortunately, the kind of thinking which is prevalent in the financial and accounting professions is the left-brain style which is not associated with visualization, innovation, entrepreneurship, or concern for people or their potential responses. It is not really their fault, in the sense that their capabilities are limited by the particular "wiring" of their brains, and if cultural trends are such that their style is in demand, can we blame them for believing that they can lead?

There are various elements of impact on a company's world which affect both the strategic and the tactical thinking of its inhabitants, particularly those in positions of influence. The degree of impact at any given time has an effect on the decisions made, and when these are of a strategic nature the results can sometimes take a long time to become apparent. Often it is too late. In order to have the right kind of decision thinking, leaders have to employ a balanced approach of the type with which geniuses like Leonardo da Vinci and Einstein were gifted.

The truth is that not too many of us can claim to have that gift. So it may be wise to appoint leaders who are humble enough to follow the example of one of the most successful entrepreneurs in business history, Andrew Carnegie. He wrote his own epitaph with the words, "Here lies a man who was wise enough to bring into his service men who knew more than he." That philosophy would fit with the advice given in the book *The Professional Decision Thinker* by Ben Heirs. He differentiates significantly between decision making and professional decision thinking and makes the point that decision thinking is not a management technique like "discounted cash flow" or "management by objectives" but is a mental process which has been implicit in *all* action-related thinking throughout human history.

Another author, Alistair Mant, in his book *Leaders We Deserve*, refers to the crisis of leadership caused by too many people, particularly the young, realizing you don't have to obey inadequate authority figures. If the authority figures in organizations are perceived as inadequate, it is often because of their failure to involve their own experienced people in the decision-thinking process as recommended by Heirs. If those same experienced people feel that they and their knowledge of the business are not valued, they do not feel inclined to support the leaders. Napoleon, one of history's inspirational leaders, made it his business to make his men feel valued and individually important. Before he carried out inspections, he would find out about the personal things that were going on in the lives of his troops and ask them about these things. The return on that small investment of time was enormous in terms of loyalty and effort he received from them

In answer to the question, "How do you recognize a good manager?" a highly respected associate of mine replied:

> A good manager knows what's going on:
> - with the business,
> - with the marketplace, and
> - with the people.
>
> They keep themselves fully aware of all the things that matter to the business all the time, and they use that information to their advantage. They may not always get everything right every time, but they don't get many nasty surprises—they give themselves opportunity to minimize potential problems.

A leader can have tremendous advantage from knowing what is going on in the way the key people in the business think, that is, from knowing their *preferred thinking style*. Because of the relative shortage of "Leonardos" and the value of good decision thinking as described by Ben Heirs, a wise leader will ensure that there is a good balance of perceptions of the pros and cons to the organization when any proposals for significant changes or innovations are being considered.

An individual's preferred thinking style has a direct effect on the importance he or she attaches to various aspects of any situation or dilemma. The left-brained pragmatist will be most concerned about how something will work, how quickly there will be a good return on the investment, how easy it will be to implement, and how much it will cost. The right-brained entrepreneur will be concerned about its possibilities for the future, the stimulus it will provide, being ahead of the competition, and the prospects of high rewards. The pragmatist will also probably have loads of historical data which can be useful in order to avoid falling into costly traps from previous experience whilst the entrepreneur most likely will have a good instinct for the likely effect on the other people involved. How many costly mistakes have been made because the decision maker did not have the right decision thinking beforehand? In other words, the best leaders arm themselves with knowledge of how their top teams will be looking at issues, and they know they will receive well-balanced information which will form the basis of their own decision making, provided they have ensured that the other thinkers are quite clear about the purpose of their deliberations.

One instrument I use for this task of putting together well-balanced teams and for identifying the strengths and weaknesses of thinking styles for particular jobs is a document called a "BrainMap" devised by Dudley Lynch of Brain Technologies Corporation.

In all of my training workshops, this is by far and away the most enthusiastically received topic in the program. It also tells me very much about how I should be expressing things to ensure I can "tune in to" all of the participants because I am armed with the knowledge of the things to which each of them will respond positively. It is a marvelous aid to communication, and this means that everyone will give proper consideration to whatever I am dealing with because I am talking about it in their terms, and they are then more receptive. On these occasions, the clarity of purpose is more likely then to be collective.

In companies, when the clarity of purpose is collective, and has been periodically reviewed and arrived at in a participative culture, it is much more likely to be not only understood but accepted by the organization as a whole. How then does an organization attempt to attain this clarity of purpose in a hectic and ever-changing business world in which they need everyone to be personally effective? How, in fact, does an individual know how to make the best contribution to the company's purpose?

The questions we have to ask ourselves if we need to be sure of our personal effectiveness within our own company are sometimes found in good appraisal systems, but, as yet, not in all. You may decide to ask them of yourself:
- How clear am I about the purpose of my organization?
- What are the current goals of the company in performance terms?
- Do I know which direction we are going in the marketplace?
- Do I understand what my own contribution to the market plan is?
- Have I agreed to any objectives to make that contribution a reality?
- Do I feel that my colleagues also understand these things?

If we cannot answer these questions reasonably positively, then the clarity of purpose is lacking. Even if it has been expressed at some level, if it has not been universally understood, then the communication system to some extent negates it.

There is an amusing little adage about the man with no purpose or direction:

> He didn't know where he was going.
> When he got there, he didn't know he had arrived.
> When he got back, he didn't know where he had been.

How many of us can identify with that man? I would suggest too many. In my days as a training adviser to companies who wanted to create or improve training systems, I would frequently be involved in helping them to produce job definitions.

My approach would be to question the people who carried out particular jobs about their understanding of what was required of them as well as asking the same questions to the managers to whom they reported. It never ceased to amaze me how much disparity there was between the descriptions offered from each party about the same job. How was anything ever achieved? The tragedy was that invariably both worked quite hard, but the outcomes from their efforts were never as satisfactory as they might have been.

A question I frequently ask is, "What is the purpose of any manager, at any level, in any company, of any size, in any sector, in any country?—Answer in only four words please." In probably 99 percent of the responses, people offer all sorts of "doing" words that include many of the skills which managers must have in order to fulfill their purpose, but the four words I look for are: "**to achieve desired results**."

Those desired results should be the department's contribution to the achievement of the company's goals for whatever period during that manager's employment. That is why the manager is there, and within this the manager's key responsibility is to achieve the best return on the resources invested in that department.

Whether we like it or not, the main purpose for a business (but not necessarily an institution) is **not** to keep people in employment, nor to serve the community. These are benefits which a business can create. Their purpose is to provide products or services for which there is a market and which they can profitably supply, within the parameters of legal trading. If they are a non-profit-making entity, then their purpose may be described somewhat differently.

The profits derived should be sufficient to create an acceptable return so that the organization can continue to serve the marketplace, maintain jobs, and in so doing benefit the community in some way. I hope that this demonstrates the importance of clarity of purpose for the leaders and managers of businesses, but it should also be remembered that each of us working in them bears the same sort of responsibility for maintaining the prosperity of our own organization. However, if the leadership and the communication style do not engender a sense of belief in acceptance of personal responsibility within the culture, then the purpose is not a shared one.

If we return to the previously mentioned elements of impact, it could be useful to imagine any company as being a little world in a universe of business. The main elements of impact could be stars whose influence variously pulls the company world in different directions, altering its course accordingly. If the company world cannot maintain its equilibrium, then it is in danger of disappearing into an abyss.

The challenge of maintaining the equilibrium of an organization and minimizing the negative impact of influences outside its own sphere of control, whilst simultaneously guiding the necessary initiatives and innovation to sustain competitiveness, is the real test of leaders in business. One of the most helpful things those leaders can have is their own *clarity of purpose*, and for ourselves as individuals this is equally true.

You may find the following format for a top team workshop a very useful tool which you could use in a do-it-yourself approach or, even better, with the help of a good facilitator who will coordinate your efforts.

I have named it a "Business Definition Workshop" for reasons which will become obvious when you study it.

BUSINESS DEFINITION WORKSHOP

The purpose of this workshop is to devise a new "Statement of Intent" for the company. The first thing we have to decide is:

What "business" are we in?
(What is our purpose in the marketplace?)

Step 1
We will examine our current business operation and its relevance to global trends as well as its culture; we will evaluate it, highlight our opportunities for the future, and decide:

What business shall we be in from now on, and how will we conduct ourselves?

Step 2
We will then devise our strategy and tactics to take us where we want to be, taking into consideration the implications of any changes and the impact on our people:

Where we want to be becomes the company goal.

Step 3
We then involve everyone who will play a part in achieving it:
- Make sure they know how and what they have to do to make their personal contribution, and
- We know and appreciate their concerns as well as their reservations. Then, **we all go for it**!

Having clearly defined the purpose of our business, we will all be in no doubt as to why we are here, whom we are serving, and how we will operate from now on.

It can be seen that there are strategic and tactical questions that are relevant not only to new businesses, but to all business—no matter how long they have been established. Every business should have answers to each of these questions, and the answers need to be based upon coherent commercial reasons; the reasons will relate to the state of the company as a business entity today and what external elements affect it by whatever means or to whatever extent.

Example: How many operational units do you have?
            Why did you feel you needed these?
            Are your answers still valid in the current circumstances?

Although there are always factors outside their control, it is senior executives' responsibility to direct the efforts of everyone to best effect.

In order to safeguard the well-being of the business, those charged with the direction of the company must regularly carry out their own appraisal of their strategy and tactics.

It is our duty to ensure that we approach this task with complete honesty and objectivity and that we complete the task in full.

All the questions will invariably raise subsidiary questions, and almost certainly there will be areas of disagreement and priorities. This is how it should be, but we will work towards a consensus in order to complete this exercise effectively

OUR TERMS OF REFERENCE:
- There will be a clearly articulated "Statement of Intent" for the company.
- There will be a definition of the business we intend to be in.
- There will be an affirmation of the level of investment we are seeking.
- There will be a description of our growth plan for the immediate future.
- There will be a feasible arrangement for funding.
- There will be schedules of:
  - products and services,
  - markets,
  - locations,
  - physical resources, and
  - human resources.

Notice will be given to all concerned in relation to those responsible for drawing up the plan, actively implementing action requirements, and methods of progress reporting and accountability exchange.

STRATEGY FOR CHANGE

I find the whole subject of change very fascinating. Of course there is nothing new about change and mankind's ongoing need to adapt. After all, almost the first story we are told as children is the story of Adam and Eve having to suddenly pack their bags and move on from their idyllic, supremely comfortable environment to a cold, unfriendly, and harsh new world.

Could that be why people are afraid of change? For some it is a challenge, but for many it feels very threatening indeed. They prevaricate, they procrastinate, and they subconsciously hope that either it will go away, or luck will be on their side and if they do nothing they will survive. Today, these people are a major threat in business because the one unchanging constant of business life is the fact that change is here to stay. Not only is it here to stay, but the speed at which it is taking place is breathtaking.

Now that is great for those of us who like variety, pace, the thrill and excitement of a new challenge—the gamblers, the risk takers, the mountaineers who want to climb the mountain simply because it is there. But organizations are made up of different kinds of human beings, and those of us who are managers have to deal with change with that important dimension in mind. Good managers recognize the need to plan for both imposed changes and desired changes.

How do we recognize this animal, this "good manager?" Well, that is not really too easy because, as yet, it is a really uncommon sight. Neither the male nor the female of the species is too much in evidence, but, fortunately, there are a few. Watch out for them—you will notice that they have a glint in their eye. They have a purposeful way of walking—they are going somewhere. They will have a habit of looking you in the eye, and they will probably ask a lot of questions. You recognize good managers because they have an obvious sense of *awareness* and they are inquisitive. They need to be—they need to know what's going on!

What's going on with their people, their product, their customers, their industry, their competitors, the economy, the political trends, and the state of the world? Particularly in the global business environment, every one of these things could have a major impact on their success (or for some, their survival). Therefore, they have to be "switched on" in order to have the right cards to play in the competitive game of business and the right facts on which to base their strategic or day-to-day business decisions at crucial times. They are proactive—they have a sense of urgency when it is appropriate not to wait to see what happens. They recognize the need for vision, and they plan to make their visions become reality; they are not gamblers, they are strategists. They rarely look back—they look forward—but they have the habit of learning from their mistakes, using the lessons of the past as the sources of information they need to avoid repeating mistakes. So, how do they demonstrate their proactive qualities?

They have strategic plans that they monitor and review regularly, but they are not hidebound by the plans. They know how to be flexible when exigencies demand it, whilst keeping their vision of the future. The strategy for change takes a number of things into consideration:

- The nature of the desired change
- The potential impact on the business
- The financial implications
- The resource implications
- The logistical implications
- The timescale and the critical path to the "new day"

The things that are within the manager's control can be handled and are fairly predictable, but because of the fear element, or complacency, or laziness, the unpredictable aspect can be the human resource implications. The attainability and capability of machines, money, premises, and so forth, can invariably be measured, but the commitment and co-operation of people must often be an act of faith or excellent leadership.

Many well-intentioned managers come to grief in their change strategies because they have paid insufficient attention to the prevailing environment within their organizations, particularly in respect of the nature of the change they wish to implement.

They decide (often after some "brainwashing" from a very convincing consultant or perhaps from attendance at an awareness-raising seminar) that things should change, and they should change! A new management style will be adopted. People will be given more information; they will start to work to objectives and budgets; they will become more accountable; they will take part in the decision making. All pretty good stuff!!

The problem is that many of the people working in the organization in which these envisaged changes will be innovations are working there because they have not been expected to do these things. There has been a state of symbiosis in the prevailing environment, a relationship of mutual dependence. Management has felt okay in the controlling parent role, and the workforce has had no sense of responsibility for the success or failure of the company. Middle management has consisted mainly of people who have been technically competent and loyal but have never really questioned the decisions or effectiveness of the senior management group. I have deliberately not referred to them as a team because the *Parent/Child* symbiotic environment is not one in which good teams flourish. In fact, the opposite is the case.

In an *Adult* environment in which there is mutual respect for the importance of each individual and his or her particular contribution, there is an acknowledgement of the need to share information and recognition of the importance of trust, integrity, and open honesty.

In a *Parent/Child* society, people manipulate and compete for the approval and the favor of the controlling parent. They also use that parent as their role model, and the pattern repeats and is replicated throughout the establishment.

Goods things flourish in groups that have an atmosphere of excitement—some people call it a "buzz," but you never feel that buzz in a wholly autocratic organization. At best, there is an atmosphere of compliance and control—at worst, you can detect either apathy or tension. Those discordant attitudes that emanate from negative emotions consume the energy that could have the potential to greatly increase enthusiastic productivity. When they do not experience a sense of involvement in the decisions and activities that control their lives, people will either feel resentful or they will not care at all. In Eric Berne's theory of transactional analysis, this is known as the "adapted child syndrome," an "ineffective ego state" (either compliant or rebellious) which is in evidence throughout the working relationships.

Good teams are motivated by effective ego states: *Adult* when they are required to participate in ways based on their experience, skill, and knowledge; *Natural Child* which is creative, open, transparent, and uncomplicated when enjoying the fun and excitement of participating in the creation of a vision for the future; *Nurturing Parent* when a colleague is genuinely under too much pressure and would welcome a sympathetic ear or a helping hand.

However, good teams need to have a degree of stability and some sense of security derived from confidence in the availability of support and respect from associates. They then feel that it is safe to take risks or submit ideas and that their mistakes will not automatically mean that their future is in jeopardy.

If a manager wants to inspire excitement about a "new day," there has to be leadership behavior that enables others to participate in the creation of a vision that they share and feel part of knowing that their contribution is vital to its outcome. Most of all, they must feel that although it may seem like a quantum leap into the future, it is achievable.

In his book *Thriving on Chaos*, Tom Peters comments on vision. He says:
- **Effective visions are inspiring.**
- **Effective visions are clear and challenging.**
- **Effective visions make sense in the marketplace.**

The main difference between this visionary approach and the older, more traditional approach to management is that this is based on the very thing which managers used to be taught to avoid. That is the importance of emotions. Objectivity is appropriate in some circumstances and comes from the logical left brain, but faith is more likely to be heartfelt and comes from the emotional right brain as does vision. The right brain thinks in pictures and feelings; the left brain thinks in facts, words, and numbers. In his book *Emotional Intelligence*, Daniel Goleman argues that "our view of human intelligence is far too narrow, and our emotions play a far greater role in thought, decision making and individual success than is commonly acknowledged."

Where does excitement come from? What is it? It is something that is provoked by strong stimulus—it is a feeling—an emotion! Just as one feeling can induce another, motivation is a feeling that can be a spin-off of excitement, but it is not something you can wrap up or deliver; it is not something you can put in somebody's hand. It is only something you can inspire. As I said earlier, if you describe a dream and it seems attainable, and others feel that it benefits and includes them, most will feel inspired and motivated. But if it does not feel attainable to some, they will not become emotionally involved, and they will have reservations or even resist the change.

If this is the case, the strategic manager knows that to impose a sudden requirement or change will be too traumatic for some. There has to be a kind of audit of personalities involved to identify those who can support the change master and who can become part of a catalytic force necessary to produce the changed state which is envisaged. The supporters will lead the less sure and will encourage them by their confidence and excitement. They themselves, however, will need to be convinced that the organization can change. Do the chief executive and the senior management group really want to share the power? Are they mature enough and self-confident enough to truly delegate important and challenging tasks so that they can spend time looking ahead, planning, and monitoring the company's performance in the marketplace?

These are the fundamental issues that have to be addressed in order to succeed in changing organizational style. The process consists of a number of growth indicators:

1.   A clear definition of the new state that has to be achieved (*The New Day; The Vision*)

2.   A profile of the required skills, personal qualities, and attitudes of the leaders who have to achieve the desired results (*The Clear Challenge*)

3.   A statement of the objectives and criteria for measuring results at every level (*The Business Reality*)

4.   An objective assessment of the current leadership, measured by:
- Level of individual contribution
- Extent of transferable skills and knowledge
- Level of emotional resilience displayed in times of pressure
- Degree of commitment to change indicated by behavior and initiatives
- Accuracy of self-knowledge and mature self-confidence in relationships *(The Inspired Example)*

5.   A schedule of improved communication activities based on an accurate "need-to-know" calendar *(Briefings)*

6.   A program of development activities to strengthen the working relationships and monitor attitudes *(The Learning Dimension)*

7. The development of an environment in which individual contribution is recognized and there is a climate where people will exchange good strokes (appreciation and acknowledgement) for their good performance and co-operation *(The Team Spirit)*

In brief, what is needed to implement change for long-term effectiveness?
- **The vision of the future**
- **The awareness of the leadership challenge**
- **The defined desired results**
- **The identification of achievement capabilities**
- **The appropriate communication system**
- **The learning program**
- **The "coaching for contribution" environment**

No one pretends that these things are easily achieved, but when you have, your future will be assured—it is worth trying!

QUOTES

"The psychic task which a person can and must set for himself is not to feel secure but to be able to tolerate insecurity."

Erich Fromm

"When change is successful, we look back and call it growth."

Unknown

Strategic and Tactical Questions

Today—The Present

1. What business are we in today? (Does our mission statement reflect this?)
2. Who are our customers? (What market are we in?)
3. Who are our competitors?
4. What business are they in?
5. How well are we doing?
6. How do we compare with our competitors?
7. How could we improve?
8. Is our location appropriate?
9. Should we have more units?
10. Are our systems and methods effective?
11. What motivates our people?
12. How would we describe our prevailing environment (the business culture)?
13. Do we need to change?

Tomorrow—The Future

14. What business will we be in?
15. Who will be our customers?
16. How will they recognize us?
17. Where will we be located?
18. How will we be structured?
19. What are the manpower implications?
20. What investment(s) will be needed?
21. Can this be made available?
22. What return on investment will we require?
23 What kind of prevailing environment will we need?
24. What are the development implications in human resource terms?
25. Do we need to change our systems?
26. How proactive will we have to be in terms of increasing our revenue and making effective use of funding for statutory responsibilities?
27. How will we reward our people for special contributions?

Action—Our Commitment Schedule

28. Where will we start?

29. How will we start?

30. Who will be responsible?

31. What criteria will we set for judging our success?

32. How will we monitor progress?

33. What are our specific objectives?

34. What is our time schedule for our critical path?

35. Do these answers constitute our action plan?

36. Are we truly committed, and are we prepared to show our commitment by accepting accountability for part of the plan?

CHAPTER 2

Tenet Number 2—Knowledge and Best Use of Resources

"Superior leaders get things done with very little motion. They impart instruction not through many words, but through a few deeds. They keep informed about everything but interfere hardly at all. They are catalysts, and though things would not get done as well if they weren't there, when they succeed they take no credit. And because they take no credit, credit never leaves them."

Lao-Tzu

There is often reference to the difference between leaders and managers, and there is no doubt that this is significant. There is also, however, an equally significant common requirement, and that is their need for awareness of the resources at their disposal and their ability to make best use of them.

In business, the potential list of resources is quite long, and possibly this is why best use of them is not always made. In order to successfully operate an enterprise, no matter how large or how small, knowledge and best use of the following are vital:

- Optimum working capital
- Necessary competencies at all levels
- Appropriate technology
- Efficiency of equipment and machinery
- Existing and potential customer base
- Operational systems
- Caliber and accessibility of suppliers
- Sources of relevant knowledge and expertise
- Quality of working relationship with bankers
- Levels of commitment and morale
- Prevailing culture and environment
- Sources of additional funds
- Information on best practices
- Opportunities for productive collaborations
- Application of capabilities

It could be said that no one person could easily maintain an up-to-date knowledge of all of the above, but Einstein had a very good answer to this. He did not see the need to carry too much minutiae in his head, but he did make sure that he knew where to access it when necessary. This is also the message in Ben Heirs' philosophy of participative decision thinking. The right team, with a common purpose and a consciousness of the value of their particular area of contribution, will invariably provide the necessary knowledge of resources when and where needed. The best leaders then, like Andrew Carnegie, whose life progressed from being the son of a poor Scottish immigrant to becoming one of America's richest and most famous entrepreneurs, surround themselves with the right people, carefully chosen to create a well-balanced team.

Carnegie had the admirable kind of self-confidence that enabled him to acknowledge the strengths and contributions of others when he famously composed his own epitaph referred to earlier.

Bringing the right people into your service, of course, starts with the selection process, and there are many services available to help with the task of attracting candidates. The candidates themselves also have access to help in their task of presenting themselves in the best possible light. This means that in terms of identifying previous experience, qualifications, and even details of achievements, it is really an administrative process of sifting. What is frequently ignored by both parties, however, is the importance of "fit." By that I mean the expectations on both sides of what represents a satisfactory working environment. The *prevailing environment* of a working group emanates from the management style and the ethos of the organization. This is usually referred to as *the culture*; if the expectations do not match, the relationship will never fully blossom, and even the most suitably qualified person will often be a disappointment. Quite frequently, in these circumstances, they will leave by their own volition if they are not dismissed. A good team can be diminished by being joined by someone whose values are different from the majority, and a very competent person can become a failure by being in the wrong place. It is therefore important to explore values and expectations of working relationships when making important selection decisions. Finding the right people can be a very time-consuming process, but it is well worth the effort if you want to have winners.

Any football fan will tell you, however, that it is not enough to have a group of *stars* available to play for the team. If you want to have consistently winning performance, the manager must know how to make best use of their talents, both individually and collectively. Just as investment in the very latest technology is wasted if the operators are not competent to use it or if it is inappropriate for the needs of the business in terms of capacity or finished product, the selection and deployment of people is a crucial management responsibility.

One feature of management still too prevalent in the United Kingdom is the expectation that training is an unnecessary luxury for managers. My own rather tongue-in-cheek way of describing this is that there is an ongoing belief in fairies in British business culture. We have all heard of the *tooth fairy* who visits us in the night when we have just lost our first baby tooth which, if placed under our pillow, will magically become money. Well, there appears to be another even more benevolent creature, the *management fairy*, who visits those who have just been appointed to their first management position. When they fall asleep on the first night following the confirmation of their new status, she waves her magic wand over them, and from that moment on they think strategically, plan and organize efficiently, become superb judges of people and situations, are experts in the financial structure and performance of any business, and are expert decision makers.

We all know that is rubbish, but on the one hand we have managers who appear to believe it themselves and on the other, even worse, we have senior executives who repeatedly block or ignore requests from people—from whom they expect superior performance—for the kind of training or coaching that they need. To some extent, this is understandable in smaller companies where the absence of a few people for learning activities can mean very significant pressure on those "holding the fort," but it is an important management challenge in itself to make allowance for this when producing business plans and budgets. Britain cannot afford to keep maintaining the cult of *glorious amateurs*. After all, if the head of a business buys an expensive new car, it is an unquestioned expectation that resources will be allocated to provide the regular servicing that will be required in order to ensure it continues to perform at the highest level. Why should this not also apply to people?

If people are not equipped to do what is required of them, then there is more pressure on the leader to find ways of compensating for the inabilities, and this is one reason why, often around the third year of operation, some promising businesses fail. The more successful they have been in their early days, the more likely it is that they have been lulled into a false sense of security about their prospects. The heady excitement of increasing sales, together with the admiration being heaped upon them, blinds them to the reality that the business is becoming a different entity. Wise operators recognize the importance of regular reviews of policies, practices, systems, and people to ascertain where and when changes should take place. Without this, decline almost inevitably results, sometimes gradually and sometimes very suddenly.

Although it is of great importance to equip the business with the very best material and physical resources and to obtain the best possible financial support available, this will

KNOWLEDGE AND BEST USE

be to no avail if the people who have to manage and operate them are not themselves equipped appropriately. If a leader needs to delegate, as is inevitable in the task of ensuring knowledge and best use of the resources of the organization as a whole, then delegation itself must be understood. We must recognize the difference between *delegation* and *abdication*. The good leader does not abdicate when handing over responsibilities but retains joint accountability for outcomes. As Truman famously said, "The buck stops here." And it does, but that does not mean that the leader does all the "doing." There are some rules about delegating that are worth recalling here, so forgive me if you have seen them before, but good rules are always worth the recall. First of all, we must be clear about a definition of delegation. To delegate is *to entrust to the care of another some specific obligation*. To do this responsibly and avoid abdication, there are certain requirements. There should be:

- A clear statement of the task or responsibility
- A timescale for results or reporting
- Provision of the necessary resources
- Clarity of constraints and limits of authority

By fulfilling these requirements, the leader will be:

- Establishing a clear contract
- Transferring initiative, responsibility, and authority for agreed tasks
- Retaining and exercising the right to monitor agreed performance

What the leader should also do, however, is support the person to whom this trust has been given but also allow him or her to grow. There are a number of actions that can be taken to encourage this growth:

- Build up confidence in the colleague.
- Have clear lines of command.
- Delegate the end result rather than the method of achieving it.
- Involve the colleague in the process of delegation by discussion and agreement.
- Agree on priorities and any deadlines after discussions.
- Record what has been agreed.
- Having delegated the necessary authority, inform other interested parties in order to avoid misunderstandings which could undermine the colleague's ability to succeed.
- Be available to discuss serious problems and assist decision making but avoid being the provider of the solutions.
- Be convinced that the person has the necessary experience and personal qualities to cope with the new challenges and express your confidence in him or her.
- Allow any necessary training to take place which will enhance the person's likelihood of success.

No one can reasonably be held accountable if they are unable, through no fault of their own, to deliver the desired results. It could then be argued that personal and staff competence is *the* most important criterion in judging management performance. In other words, it is the element of management that ultimately makes the difference between success and mediocrity. Yet it is so often the element that is left to chance or is locked in that *good intentions box*. It *is* going to happen—but not today! So the workers keep battling away with their inferior resources until they are too tired, dispirited, or disillusioned to keep performing as they did.

In a later chapter we will explore the subject of morale maintenance, but in the meantime the issue of criteria for judging the caliber of managers is one of critical importance. There are five elements which should always be included in the appraisal of any manager:
- Personal motivation
- Resource management
- Decision making
- Interpersonal skills
- Expertise development

Many people claim that it is very difficult to be objective about performance in these areas, but you may like to use the following descriptions of management behavior. These are arranged in descending order starting with the ideal performer through to the manager who is in the wrong job. You might even decide to rate yourself!

Each of the following can be allocated a score between 5 and 0 with a score of 5 representing the ideal. (There will not be too many of us who could fall into this category, but we can all aspire to it!!). A total score of 25 will indicate that this person is a fully effective manager. A score of less than 10 suggests that this person has been promoted well beyond his or her capabilities and will not only be failing to fulfill his or her responsibilities, but will, in all likelihood, be leading a group of people who are not being enabled to contribute all that they are capable of. The final failure then is that of the leader who allows such a situation to continue.

KNOWLEDGE AND BEST USE

PERSONAL MOTIVATION

Score	Explanation
5	The manager energetically initiates activities to deal with challenging situations, or projects, immediately upon identifying the requirements or benefits of addressing them, frequently setting personal goals for achievement of high results.
4	The manager responds quickly to requests for attention to identified priority situations, frequently finding ways of accommodating these without neglecting other demands.
3	The manager can be depended upon to carry out the responsibilities of the job with diligence, setting priorities in order to maintain necessary control over critical issues.
2	The manager maintains laid-down systems and procedures, using personal authority to delegate the initiation of new activities to others.
1	The manager sometimes takes avoiding action to avert changes or disruption to routine procedures, failing to recognize signals of complacency or decline in performance.
0	The manager is failing to respond to indicators of the need for innovation or preventive action, resulting in unacceptable performance from self or department.

RESOURCE MANAGEMENT

Score	Explanation
5	The manager clearly demonstrates awareness of the requirement to obtain maximum return on investment in all resources, taking steps to identify capabilities, utilizing productivity potential, and obtaining best performance from every available element of cost.
4	The manager identifies the strengths and limitations of people, location, technology, and equipment and delivers outcomes which ensure that the department contributes to profitability.
3	The manager operates within all budgeted expenditure limits and obtains satisfactory performance from all available resources.
2	The manager is not able to provide evidence of acceptable performance from available resources that justify the costs incurred by the department.

I	The manager regularly incurs unbudgeted costs due to unforeseen failures of people, equipment, communication, and/or necessary expertise in self or others.
0	The manager does not deliver optimum results from available resources and so fails to justify higher-than-expected departmental costs or lower-than-required performance.

DECISION MAKING

Score	Explanation
5	The manager displays ability to differentiate between strategic decisions requiring time and data before implementation, and tactical decisions to be made rapidly in response to the need for operational effectiveness. The majority of decisions made have beneficial consequences.
4	The manager is able to make decisions with confidence and recognizes those situations when opinions, expertise, or experience are important in order to obtain best consequences.
3	The manager is able to make decisions which can be justified in the light of commercial and operational outcomes.
2	The manager is occasionally hesitant about important decisions and prefers to seek guidance before becoming accountable for outcomes.
I	The manager frequently avoids making decisions and thereby delays or hinders the ability of others to take specific action at times of uncertainty.
0	The manager invariably refers to laid-down procedures or higher authority before giving direction to others or clarifying areas of uncertainty.

INTERPERSONAL SKILLS

Score	Explanation
5	The manager has unfailing ability to inspire others to give full commitment to group success, resulting in consistently higher-than-expected performance from all peers and associates.
4	The manager has the ability to obtain the cooperation of others and can clearly convey confidence in associates to deliver high performance. Collective efforts frequently result in higher-than-required results.
3	The manager displays ability to obtain group achievement of set goals and tasks by articulating and acknowledging the individual contribution of all associates.

KNOWLEDGE AND BEST USE

Score	Explanation
2	The manager fails to adequately clarify desired results or display confidence in group's ability to deliver high performance, so producing lower levels of achievement than expected capability.
1	The manager fails to obtain expected levels of performance from associates. Staff turnover and stability levels indicate low morale and higher-than-appropriate recruitment and training costs.
0	There are regular instances of misunderstandings and poor communication within the manager's sphere of influence and control.

EXPERTISE DEVELOPMENT

Score	Explanation
5	The manager accepts responsibility for identification of the degrees of knowledge, skill, and potential available within self and associates. In relation to present and future needs of the organization, all possible steps are taken to appraise and facilitate best performance and opportunities for learning, A coaching style of management is used which includes two-way feedback.
4	The manager carries out regular appraisals to identify competencies, training needs, and development aspirations of associates, willingly sharing knowledge as a means of coaching others. Training is implemented to meet specific job requirements, and there is encouragement of the exchange of knowledge and insights within the department as a whole.
3	The manager fulfills the company requirements to conduct annual appraisals and takes the appropriate steps to follow up in terms of any action agreed to satisfy training needs.
2	The manager restricts appraisals to the assessment of current job performance and sometimes allows excessive time to elapse before taking action to facilitate learning or deliver training.
1	The manager spends only minimum time on appraisals and regularly fails to follow up apparent performance-related training needs.
0	The manager fails to take the necessary steps to identify training and development needs or show interest in staff problems.

No matter how large or how small a company is, that set of performance indicators for management is wholly applicable. The best use of resources is the true pathway to profitability, and profitability is the key to sustainable growth. It is a fool's paradise to believe that borrowing is always likely to be possible. It can be a way of getting started, but investors and lenders will, quite rightly, always have the right to demand repayment. If a company is overburdened with debt, its ownership is actually in the hands of the lenders, so it is always vulnerable. Self-financed growth is one of the best objectives a management team can have.

Wise entrepreneurs will learn the importance of good financial management and will listen to the counsel of a competent financial colleague. They may not always agree in the decision-making process, but they should be able to communicate and voice their reservations with mutual respect. The risk element of the ultimate decisions will be clarified, and the leader will be taking a calculated risk rather than a gamble.

The responsibility for monitoring our original list of resources can be delegated, and in a later chapter we will look at a simple way the leader can maintain an up-to-date awareness of the performance in all of those areas of the business.

KNOWLEDGE AND BEST USE

CHAPTER 3

Tenet Number 3—Focus on Critical Success Factors

"To lead to immediate action, control information has to be simple and obvious, whether on the shopfloor or in the boardroom. Top management does not normally have the time to analyse pages of figures. It needs to see a brief summary from which it can extract at a glance what is going right or wrong."
The Winning Streak Workout Book, by Walter Goldsmith and David Clutterbuck

People who travel about the country in the course of their work probably spend quite a lot of time in hotels either attending meetings or simply finding refreshment during journeys. They could not fail to notice that in most of these establishments on any day of the week, there appears to be some kind of conference or training activity in evidence. If they also frequent bookshops, they will also see many shelves devoted to the subject of management. From both of these observations, it could be assumed that the fundamentals of good management are becoming increasingly well understood and practiced. Yet it never ceases to astound me how often I find that the most paramount rule of good management is the one that is most commonly broken. As we all know, the golden rule is that managers must *communicate*, and, of course, most of them truly believe that they do.

What they do not appear to understand is that communication has not taken place if the receiver of information has *not fully understood* the message that the sender believes has been transmitted. This is excellently demonstrated in the poster which is often seen in card shops which says, "I know you believe you understand what you think I said, but I'm not sure you realize that what you heard is not what I meant." Too many of us assume that if we have mentioned something in passing, or even relayed some information in a meeting, by memo, or on a notice board, we have communicated. What we usually fail to do is check for mutual understanding. In the normal course of things, this is not the end of the world. People work things out for themselves, and life goes on. In the highly competitive business world of today, however, this can lead to disaster.

Imagine a scenario in which the heads of a business decide that they need to take themselves away from the business for a few days in order to review their current situation, future prospects, and way forward. They spend their days away laboriously analyzing, brainstorming, strategizing, devising, and finalizing. At the end of all this work, they feel pretty exhausted but convinced they have the formula for success that will take the company into a bright future. They will have set goals, maybe even formulated an impressive mission statement, identified their strengths and weaknesses, and agreed upon action plans. They can now go back to the workplace with clear consciences about their absence and the cost of the exercise. After all, they have just been taking part in a very, very important activity: setting the future direction of the company.

The problem is that, having completed this task, there appears somehow, too often, a conviction that it will now happen. What they do not demonstrate is their awareness that, to borrow someone else's phrase, "the map is not the territory." They fail to take sufficient time to follow up their conference by carrying out the actions which will ensure that their plans will have the best possible chance of becoming reality.

Those closest to them on a daily basis will have a reasonable chance of hearing the outcomes of their deliberations and maybe even be given the task of letting other members of the working group know what was decided. The mission statement will be printed, framed, and hung up in the reception area so that all visitors will know how professional they are. The company goals will be printed in the company newsletter or on posters on the cafeteria walls so everyone will know what has to be achieved, and yet, and yet—!

Unless every individual can relate his or her own efforts directly to these goals, energy will be dissipated in other directions. Even though people are working hard and feel a sense of commitment to the organization, their collective results are far from what could be. There are seven deadly killers to individual contribution:
- **"I don't know what's wanted."**
- **"I don't know what others know."**
- **"I don't know my contribution, but I know my strengths, and I can beat those others."**
- **"I want to help, but I'm not sure how I can."**
- **"I think the boss knows and might let me in on it soon— maybe!"**
- **"Sometimes I find out at the cafeteria or at the office party when the boss has had a few drinks—but I don't know whether he's serious or not."**

The senior management team needs to put in place, and treat as a major priority, some processes for ensuring that their desired results, simply expressed, are properly understood by those who will carry out the activities which will make the difference between success and failure. People need to be able to relate their own jobs and tasks to the company goals. They need to understand the importance of doing the right things, especially at those times when there are conflicting demands on their time and energy. They need to acknowledge the difference between *efficiency* and *effectiveness* (efficiency is doing things in the right way, effectiveness is getting the right things done) as well as knowing what are the *critical success factors* of both their department and their own job in that department. Efficiency is a major contributor to effectiveness, but many incredibly efficient people and departments are "beavering" away at the wrong things because current priorities have changed but this has not been made clear to them. They are not aware of those things which have become critical to the health, stability, and competitiveness of the business.

What is fundamental is the acceptance of the requirement to clearly demonstrate the hierarchy of goals from the top down and the bottom up. When people cannot see the relevance of what they do to the ultimate success of the business, there is no consciousness of the significance of either their attitudes or their actions. If managers do not feel the need to properly communicate with their people, they themselves are dismally ignorant of what their own priorities are. Mike Davidson expresses this well in *The Grand Strategist* when he states, "Organisations do not take action, people do. And people only implement what they are involved in creating." Some of the most junior staff can have the answer to major problems, but they often feel invisible. Let me give an example:

If I am responsible for sending out invoices, and the details on a dispatch note do not agree with an original order form (which was not fully completed in any case), I will, because I try very hard to be efficient, take time out to try to resolve the query. The invoice, which is for a considerable amount of money, is now delayed, but the goods have been dispatched. My colleague who made the successful sale is away enjoying a rewarding holiday for achievement of high sales targets, but, as is frequently the case, is not available to clarify those important details. The invoice will have to go with the others that are also in the queries tray. The financial controller has been at the next desk telling another colleague to hold back payments to our suppliers as we have some temporary cash flow problems. This seems to be happening quite often lately, and I cannot understand it because we must be making lots of money with all these sales. I wish I could get all those invoices out, but that salesman seems to think it doesn't matter if the order forms are wrong as long as the sales are in the bag and the customers get their stuff on time. I wonder if I should mention it to someone? The trouble is all the bosses are very busy with their meetings and everything, and there are not very many opportunities to talk to them or ask about these kinds of things. It'll probably be alright because if it was really important something would have been said by now.

Does that sound like an improbable scenario, or does it sound uncomfortably familiar? Those who have experienced severe financial pressures will already have taken steps to make everyone aware of the *critical* importance of efficiency in the administration of sales and accounting procedures. This is because of the direct and immediate effect that these have on the financial health of the business, but there are still those who have blind spots about administration. Unfortunately, it is all too common a characteristic found in salespeople. They tend to believe that selling is the most important activity in the business and time spent on administration is a loss of good selling time. (Somebody else can sort out minor details!) What the true professional recognizes is that a sale only has final value when it has been paid for in full and on time. It follows then that a critical success factor for salespeople is the level of profitability deriving from their sales achievements. The sales are merely a means to an end, not an end in themselves. This can be a revelation for some.

The principle of critical success factors applies throughout the business and should be applied as the key element of performance management of both departments and individuals.

All chief executives will have their own critical success factors whether they recognize them as such or not. Up-to-date information on those things which indicate the state of the business should, at any given moment, be available. The important thing to remember is the word *critical*. Too much data is the danger that today's technology can present within management information systems. Multitudes of reports and lengthy columns of figures can be a statistician's dream but an entrepreneur's nightmare. The eyes glaze over, and the mind wanders on to more stimulating activities because somebody has forgotten the "need to know rule." What information is really needed to monitor priorities; how and when should this be highlighted and to whom?

Examples of the things which the average chief executive would have on his or her short list of critical success factors would invariably include:

CASH FLOW	Can the company pay its creditors as necessary as well as the salaries of its employees and any other statutory obligations without breaching any loan agreements with its bankers?
DEBT RATIO	How much of the capital used to fund the operation is from external sources, loans and so forth, compared to income generated from trading profitably, and how do these compare at specific times?
BOTTOM-LINE PROFIT	Are the monthly comparisons of income and expenditure indicating a trend towards the likely achievement of the planned profit needed to reinvest in the business and provide a satisfactory return to the shareholders?
MARKET SHARE	How does the company's sales performance compare with that of its competitors over a specific period, and is the trend positive or negative?

Obviously, the list for any chief executive would bear a distinct relationship to the stated goals in a given period of the company planning, but, as the ongoing health and stability of the organization is inherently a major responsibility, ignoring those mentioned would be extremely unwise.

It is then apparent that every department in the business can affect at least some, if not all, of these components, so critical success factors would permeate throughout all operational groups and individuals. Each one needs to be made accountable for a particular contribution to ultimate success in order that the key measures of the company's performance can be maintained at the right level.

For each part of the business (that is, departments, units, or individuals), there are one or two indicators as to the areas of contribution that would make the crucial difference. These are those critical things that really matter to the business which must be achieved by everyone involved within the network. There is a state of mutual dependency between departments which dictates that failure or delay in one of them inevitably makes it difficult or sometimes even impossible for others to fulfill their roles adequately. So the proverbial "rotten apple" can spoil the barrel that is the group endeavor!

In other words, every operational element has its own set of critical success factors. These elements are *the* most important contributors to the company's health. They need to be clearly known by everyone and agreed upon with the chief executive periodically, in line with the goals being focused upon in the current operational period. They then become constant priorities for everyone and are regularly the subject of progress reports.

Each manager agrees on these priorities for his or her own department, communicates through participative discussion with colleagues on the implications involved, and devises the simplest methods for monitoring. Experience has taught that the most efficient and therefore best methods are those which are easy to apply because they are the most likely to be adhered to in the longer term. This practice ensures that the likelihood of accurate information—at agreed, regular intervals—being available to the chief executive can be guaranteed. Reports can be daily, weekly, monthly, or quarterly as deemed necessary for the guardian of the company well-being to maintain proper control. It also then makes it possible for changes to be made at an early stage if trends are indicating danger rather than at the point when damage has already become apparent. We all know that when it comes to health, prevention is better than cure.

Maintaining the golden rule of good communication, each manager ensures that all individuals within his or her sphere of operation are aware of, and can articulate, the critical success factors that represent their personal contribution and are prepared to self-monitor the day-to-day implications.

If this can be achieved, the company will have a well-informed management team leading a highly productive workforce which has a sense of its own importance. A weekly reporting document can consist of as little as two very brief and simple pages of data known as the "**Business Focus Report**" with each department recording the current status in actual figures (or in percentages) for its own factors.

EXAMPLE BUSINESS FOCUS REPORT—SUCCESS FACTORS

Business Year

	Success Factors	Status	Goals
1	Cash Flow		
2	Debt Ratio		
3	Bottom-Line Profit		
4	Market Share		
5			
6			

EXAMPLE DEPARTMENTAL FOCUS REPORT

Week No.	Department	Critical Success Factors	Goals	Status

CHAPTER 4

Tenet Number 4—Accountability for Contribution

"Wise Chieftains grant both authority and responsibility to those they have delegated assignments...they always hold their subordinates accountable for delegated assignments. Worthy Chieftains accept full responsibility for all assignments—even those they have delegated to their subordinates."

Leadership Secrets of Attila the Hun, by Wess Roberts

It would be logical to assume that the old adage "a fair day's work for a fair day's pay" would be commonly accepted philosophy in a society that considered itself to be generally honest and hard-working. Bearing that in mind, it is surprising how little real attention is paid to the subject of accountability. It is indisputable that, in the workplace, all who receive a salary or a wage are accountable for those things which collectively constitute their job. In other words, they are responsible for ensuring that those things for which they are paid are carried out properly, accurately, and on time.

For some people, that may mean making the right strategic decisions. For others it may simply mean maintaining clean premises on a day-to-day basis. Businesses cannot and should not carry *passengers*, or people who avoid taking responsibility. In a properly managed organization, every job is there because it is a necessary part of the overall operation. Although there will always be people who have the proverbial "sloping shoulders" (they regularly manage to wriggle out of demanding situations or difficult tasks and cause their colleagues to absorb additional burdens), there is no justification for failure to address this as an issue, and failure to do so is dereliction of duty on the part of management. This has a detrimental effect on their own credibility because those who have to regularly shoulder the extra burden imposed on them by irresponsible colleagues will eventually lose respect for those managers who fail to deal with this form of dishonesty.

Although each one of us is personally responsible for our own share, productive workplaces need good teamwork if the best results are to be achieved. There is much attention paid to the importance of teaming, but amongst all the words written and spoken there is little emphasis on the accountability element. The fact that any group can be called a team does not necessarily mean that this is an accurate description of that group. If any one member does not feel accountable to the others for playing his or her part wholeheartedly, then the "team" is deficient. In this sense, accountability is a form of self-discipline. Anyone determined to avoid effort can usually find some way of shirking. Most of us will have all heard the expression "throwing a sickie," meaning taking a day off work with some trumped up illness, and those who have used this pretense never acknowledge that they are not only stealing from their employer but are abusing the tolerance of their colleagues. Either some other person has to do the work that the absentee is being paid for, or productivity suffers from delay. People who feel that they have an honest and trusting relationship with colleagues whose integrity they respect are invariably willing to put in extra effort on their behalf, and to abuse this trust is inexcusable. Nevertheless, it happens.

A good leader will eventually recognize the type of individual who always seems to have a plausible reason for not being able or available to pitch in when some extra effort is needed. This is the kind of game which, in Eric Berne's theory of transactional analysis, is known as "wooden leg"—"Oh, I would like to climb the mountain with you today, but I can't because of my wooden leg. Of course, if there's anything else I can do on another occasion, you only have to ask." For many people, the wooden leg translates as a migraine headache, a doctor's appointment at the crucial time, a chronic back problem cropping up, the child minder's timetable, and so forth.

What the leader is observing is a non-team player with a fundamentally self-centered attitude that is unlikely to change. What the leader must understand in those circumstances is that he or she is accountable to the team as a whole. The leader owes it to the rest of the group to create the kind of culture in which non-team players who have a history of convenient illnesses, as opposed to genuine episodes of sickness, are exposed when the trend is recognized. After all, the leader is also part of the team, and that part includes ensuring that each individual feels valued and is not taken for granted by any other.

Everyone must be 100 percent clear about individual and collective accountability. People must know where their personal responsibility starts and finishes, the limits of their authority and freedom to decide, as well as the equivalent for the rest of the group. If this is unclear, it leaves room for passing the buck to others and playing the kinds of games described earlier. Once again, this reinforces the message about the importance of effective communication. In a well-run workplace, there is clarity of understanding and general acceptance of levels of accountability. There is an interesting little true story that I sometimes recount to prove this point:

A London jeweler, who was totally wrapped up in his business and was normally first in and last out each day, felt unwell one afternoon and decided to go home early. About ten o'clock that evening, there was a knock on his door, and when he opened it, there stood two police constables.

"Are you Mr. X?" they inquired.

"Yes, I am," he replied.

"Are you the owner of ___ establishment?"

"Yes, I am."

"We are here to inform you that upon inspecting your premises this evening, we found them to be unsecured. The door was not locked and the security grill was not in place."

The owner, our Mr. X, had assumed that someone else would lock up, and everyone else assumed that they were not responsible but somebody else must be.

Surely, you say, this cannot be true. Unfortunately, I am assured that it is. When communication is left to assumptions and that elusive thing we call "common sense," it all too often fails us. I once had a boss who said, "The trouble with common sense is that it is not common enough!"

In some organizations this is dealt with through the use of written job definitions. These go further than job descriptions which are usually limited to a general outline of the content of the job. The main distinction of the job definition, however, is that it clearly specifies the "*measures of performance*." For each element of the job, there are related criteria for making objective judgments as to the effectiveness, or otherwise, of the job-holder's performance. In terms of communication, these are of positive help to both parties, provided that the criteria are actually measurable and observable.

There are those who claim that some aspects of work cannot be judged against measurable criteria, but I would seriously refute this. As someone who has written hundreds of job definitions for every level of job from chairman to cleaner, I know that it is perfectly possible to find ways of recognizing good from poor performance. If there is any doubt, one has only to imagine that you are paying the person from your own pocket. Then think of the things that would make you feel that you are being cheated by the person taking payment. Those will become the basis of your measures of performance. When the job definition has been perused and agreed upon, the person accepting the job is assuming accountability for the responsibilities specified and is then also able to monitor his or her own performance.

The benefits of this approach are very apparent if the company operates a formal approach to appraisal. The main concern of those who have had bad experiences of appraisal systems is that many managers have an unskilled and subjective approach to the process. Unfortunately, these concerns are not without foundation, and the damage to morale in the workplaces where this is the case is enormous. It is better not to carry out appraisals at all than it is to do it badly. Doing it badly means conducting it without proper preparation, talking at people without making any attempt to involve them in discussions, and telling them what they should be doing rather than inviting their thoughts on the current situation in their sphere of operation.

Entrepreneurs who want to grow a business into a place where people will want to work and feel valued and not a place where some privileged few carry out willful, uninformed exercise of personal power must care about the kind of culture they want to engender. They must find ways of making people feel deeply involved in their work and in relationships of mutual respect, and where accountability is a fact of life. Good performance is acknowledged, excellent performance is celebrated, and poor performance is faced and not excused unless it is out-of-character for the person involved. If a colleague is normally dependable and conscientious in his or her approach to work but starts to show less drive or commitment, this is usually an indicator that there is a problem to be addressed. The good manager who takes a pride in knowing what is going on will recognize that some tactful inquiries made to the person involved will probably create an opportunity to help in solving the problem before it becomes more widely damaging. Because that person is accountable for the responsibilities inherent in his or her job, it may be necessary to temporarily delegate some aspects to another. The good manager knows how to make those decisions and then to live by them, as well as how to handle them in such a way that everyone involved can see and understand the true motivation involved. The most important thing that has been done in those circumstances is that the responsibility for maintaining the necessary quality of performance has been accepted by the manager and has not been abdicated.

Abdication is one of the worst sins in management, and it sometimes occurs because decision making often requires courage. It can be easier to adopt a *laissez-faire* attitude in some circumstances in the hope that the problem will sort itself out if you ignore it. Some people have described their boss as "the manager in the cupboard" who spends the majority of the working day behind a closed door of an office well away from the blood and guts of the operation. These bosses are invariably the abdicators, and, unfortunately, they themselves work for other abdicators otherwise they would not continue in their positions of authority. David Freemantle in his book *Superboss* expresses it beautifully when he comments, "accountability is knowing what you'll get fired for." Abdication should be a dismissible offense! If managers are prepared to leave staff morale to chance, they should be running their own business and losing their own money, not that of the investors of the business which employs them. The people who appointed them are equally guilty if they fail to recognize and accept that they have made a bad appointment. It is not always easy to admit that you have made a mistake, but better to admit it and rectify the situation than to allow it to continue at the expense of management credibility. The higher the status of the abdicator, the more reprehensible the negligence, and, unfortunately, the easier it appears to be for that negligence to go unchecked. Directors are frequently too far removed from the pivotal parts of their enterprises to be aware of the things their peers are managing to ignore or hide. Articulate line managers can often explain away their departmental failures to meet deadlines, achieve objectives, and fulfill expectations of one kind or another, and the less assertive their peers are, the longer they can escape exposure.

Accountability takes courage and pride in the outcomes of your efforts and in the contribution you personally make to the success of your organization. It starts with the leader and permeates throughout the whole enterprise as the key indicator of the values of the organization. It should not be associated with blame as blame cultures stifle innovation and risk taking but should, more appropriately, be aligned with achievement. Risk taking, then, means that the one who is prepared to be accountable is the one who makes him or herself vulnerable. This is the mark of a true leader—those who feel accountable and are prepared to stand tall, those who do not need to maintain a low profile and hide behind others. How do you stand? As an entrepreneur, do you have sufficient belief in yourself and your values to take your ideas to the marketplace and then become the leader of a great business? Are you prepared to be selective about the kind of people you will have around you? Are you prepared to spend time learning about leadership? Do you have the integrity to fulfill your commitments to those who might back you financially or emotionally, whilst still having the courage to recognize the moment when someone has reached his or her level of incompetence and needs to be replaced? Who said it was easy? But then, if you are an entrepreneur, you will relish the challenge.

CHAPTER 5

Tenet Number 5—Optimum Risk Management

"Creating long-term success in business is a self-management process which means sustaining new habits and attitudes throughout the organisation. It's rather like slimming—the 'magic' cures don't last, only your personal determination to change succeeds in the long run."

Rosemary Harris-Loxley

A key question that has to be addressed when taking a view of the prospects of any enterprise is the likelihood of there being a well-balanced approach to nurturing it to ensure its future.

Everything in life seems to indicate that things work best when balance is maintained. My clock on the wall keeps perfect time when it hangs straight and the pendulum swings evenly. My health and well-being are maintained when I do not overindulge in my favorite foods and wines. My relationships work best when there is mutual consideration for the interests and feelings of both parties. So it is with organizations both large and small. Too much or too little emphasis on any aspect of the business operation can reduce its potential performance.

Forgive me if I use a whimsical metaphor to describe the significantly different areas of contribution that various departments make and the related characteristics of those people who work in them. Each group creates markedly interesting differences in the ambience of its department.

I have likened a company to a "world" in which someone who moves between departments is a "traveler" visiting different "lands" within it. Like the world as we know it, there are lands to the north, south, east, and west, and each of these has inhabitants who have their own languages, values, customs, and characteristics. This variety is the key to the vibrancy and evolution of that world, but as we all know it is the very thing that can also create damaging conflict. So the moral of my tale is that there is a need to make the best and most well-balanced use of the different inhabitants in any company's world, using those who can most easily interact with all as channels for communication and compatibility. It is no coincidence that my descriptions of the inhabitants relate directly to the preferred thinking styles of individuals. This can be identified using the BrainMap questionnaire available from Brain Technologies Corporation (www.braintechnologies.com) whose relevance to job aptitudes I will deal with more fully in Chapter 11 to follow.

May I now introduce you to: "The World of Business—A Traveler's Guide."

World of Business!

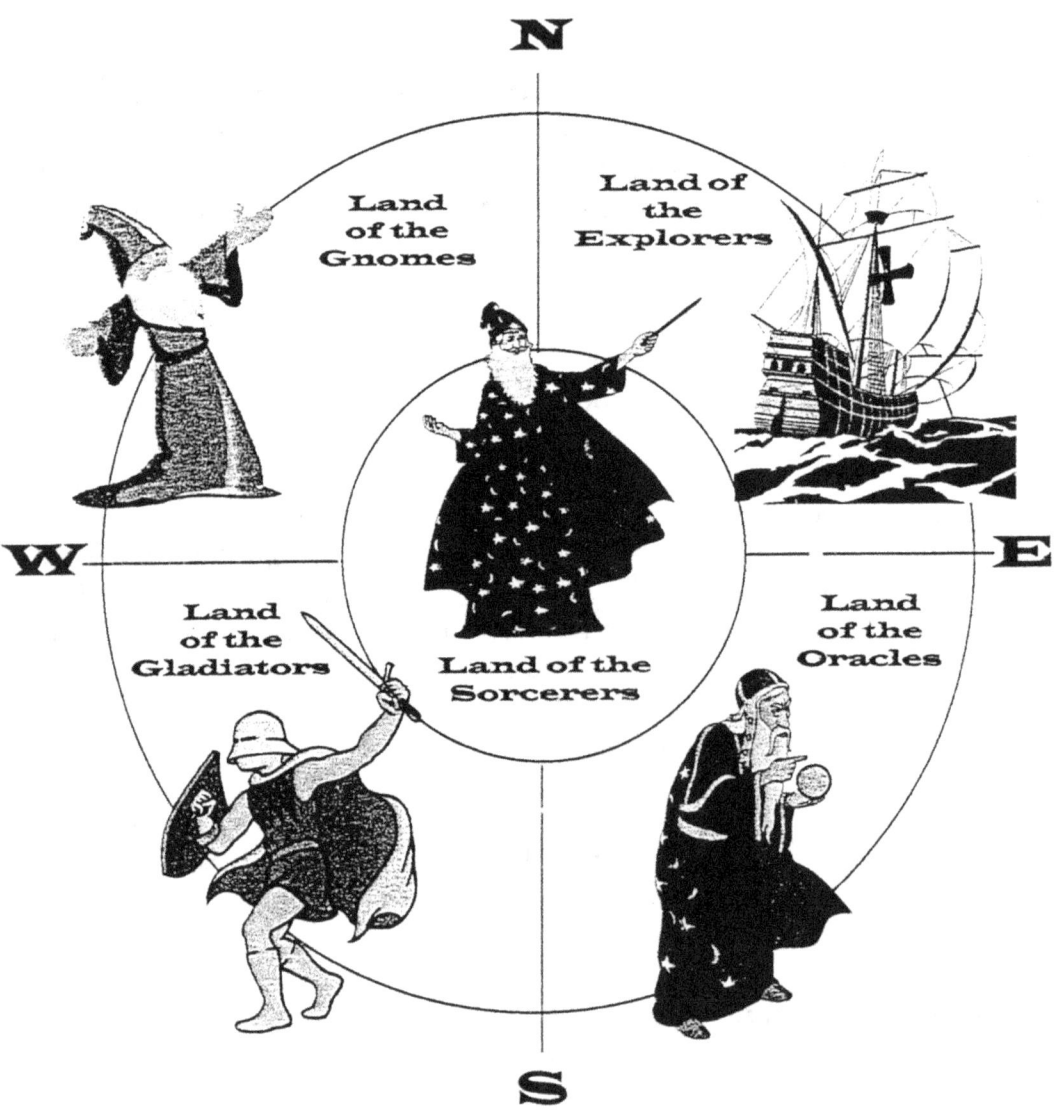

TRIP REFERENCE GUIDE

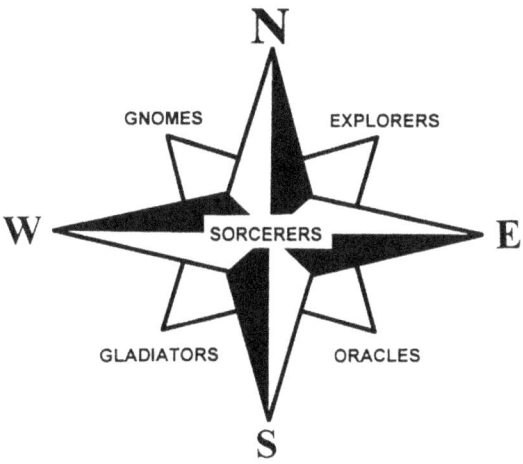

TRAVELLERS' INFORMATION ON ENVIRONMENTS TO BE EXPECTED WHILST VISITING NEW LANDS ON LEARNING TRIPS.

TRIP CATEGORIES		
INHABITANTS	**COMPASS REFERENCE**	**ENVIRONMENTS**
GNOMES	NORTH WEST	FACTUAL, TECHNICAL, RATIONAL, FINANCIAL, ANALYTICAL, LOGICAL, INTELLECTUAL, TOUGH
EXPLORERS	NORTH EAST	CREATIVE, INNOVATIVE, STRATEGIC, TRENDY, CONCEPTUAL, CHALLENGING, VISIONARY, IMPULSIVE
ORACLES	SOUTH EAST	INTUITIVE, EMPATHETIC, ENTHUSIASTIC, PERSUASIVE, EMOTIONAL, CONSIDERATE, SPIRITUAL, HELPFUL
GLADIATORS	SOUTH WEST	PRACTICAL, ACTIVE, CONSISTENT, ORDERLY, ARTICULATE, SEQUENTIAL, TRADITIONAL, RELIABLE
SORCERERS	CENTRAL	AMIABLE, ADAPTABLE, FLEXIBLE, CONCILIATORY, MODERATE, BALANCED, HARMONIOUS, REASONABLE

LEARNING TRIPS - TRAVEL CATEGORY CHECKLIST

NORTH WEST (Land of the Gnomes)

BUSINESS PLANNING (TACTICAL)
COMPANY LAW
FINANCIAL MANAGEMENT
SYSTEMS ANALYSIS
REGULATION AND STATUTORY CONTROLS
PROBLEM ANALYSIS
QUALITY SYSTEMS

TECHNICAL DESIGN
PRODUCT EVALUATION
ENGINEERING
ORGANISATION/ . DEVELOPMENT
PRODUCT DEVE_OPMENT
NETWORKING (TECHNICAL)

NORTH EAST (Land of the Explorers)

BUSINESS DEVELOPMENT (STRATEGIC)
CREATIVE THINKING
INNOVATION
CHANGE MANAGEMENT
PUBLIC RELATIONS
SALES PROMOTION
BRAIN STORMING

COACHING

RESEARCH & DEVELOPMENT
DESIGN

(Centre)

LEADERSHIP
TOTAL QUALITY
INTERNATIONAL RELATIONS
EMPOWERMENT

SALES MANAGEMENT
NEGOTIATION
PERFORMANCE APPRAISAL

SOUTH WEST (Land of the Gladiators)

FINANCIAL ACCOUNTING
P.C. LITERACY
CONTRACTUAL AGREEMENTS
ADMINISTRATION

EMPLOYMENT LEGISLATION
TECHNICAL SKILLS
PROCEDURES FORMULATION
SALARY ADMINISTRATION
PENSIONS
LANGUAGES
CREDIT CONTROL
QUALITY CONTROL
HEALTH AND SAFETY
DATA ANALYSIS
COMMERCIAL MANAGEMENT

SOUTH EAST (Land of the Oracles)

CUSTOMER SERVICE
STRESS COUNSELLING
SALES
CULTURAL ISSUES
STAFF WELFARE
NURSES
ENTERTAINMENT
CUSTOMER CARE
CONCILIATION
DISASTER RECOVERY
ETHICAL ISSUES
NETWORKING (HUMAN)

In the World of Business, different lands can be identified by the environments created by the nature of their activities, together with the behavior and attitudes of the inhabitants. The behavior of people is a reflection of the way they think, and particular styles of thinking are identifiable with the aptitudes for particular kinds of work activities.

GNOMES

In the land of finance, sometimes known as the "Land of the Gnomes," the inhabitants are much inclined to be concerned with the practicalities of business; what the value, purpose, and cost of something is, what its benefit to the business will be, and whether it will provide a measurable input into the organization within a measurable period of time. This means that their way of thinking is usually very precise, and they tend to ask a lot of questions, pressing for answers until they are satisfied that they have enough facts to enable them to make a judgment or decision. The Land of the Gnomes lies to the northwest of the World of Business, and they are noticeably different from the inhabitants of the east.

EXPLORERS

In the northeast you will encounter the land of marketing and innovation, sometimes known as the "Land of the Explorers." This is a land which is inhabited by people prone to become excited about new things to do, and they love to talk to each other about all the possibilities with which they could experiment. Sometimes they become so carried away with their ideas that they exhaust themselves, having used too many of their resources. Often, when this happens, they have to send for a Gnome because Gnomes are very good at resourcing businesses in trouble. It is not usually something they like to do because those Gnomes always ask very tricky questions, and they speak a different language than the Explorers who find them very boring and tiresome at times. They have often been at war in the past, and, try as they might, they still find it difficult to live together peacefully, so they tend to stay in their own parts of the world and avoid each other as much as possible. The Explorers think much more expansively than their Gnome neighbors who tend to be more narrowly focused on a few things at any given time.

ORACLES

The people of the northern lands are often brought together by the inhabitants of another land to the southeast of the World of Business. This is a place often visited by tourists from the rest of the world when they are troubled or unwell, or sometimes people just visit them when they want to consult an Oracle. The Oracle people have a reputation for being wise counselors although the Gnomes tend to regard them as being a bit "not in the real world" or mystical but admit that they sometimes have their uses. The Explorers usually like visiting them because they are good listeners and will often ask them, in a nice way, the kind of questions that the Gnomes would be likely to confront them with in the more brittle Gnome language that the Explorers hate. This is important when the Explorers need resources for some exciting new project and they must convince the Gnomes that these resources will be returned and increased. Many of the resources are very expensive, but the Oracles seem to know just how each Gnome and Explorer will react to the problem of negotiation and so are able to help them communicate.

GLADIATORS

Gladiators live in the southwest of the World of Business, and they are reputed for their willingness to spring into action and take risks without asking too many questions. They do not care to spend time exploring or finding out how things work as they just want to keep busy. They are the kind of people who are willing to be led by others they consider to be wiser or cleverer than they are, so the captains of their enterprises are often from another land, frequently the land of the Gnomes. The Gladiators often have to visit the land of the Oracles to recover from the wounds of battles they have to fight during projects devised by the Explorers but are somewhat under-resourced. This can be because the Explorers have high expectations, but the Gnomes, who control the financing, have stringent budgets in place. Gladiators themselves are regarded by the Gnomes as expensive resources. You will recognize the land of the Gladiators because it is a noisy, active place with many people surrounded by their weapons of war. These weapons are highly technical, and the Gladiators are quick to know whether or not they are effective during battles. Life can be very difficult for Gladiators if their weapons fail them, but they do not give up easily and often find very ingenious ways of winning, even with inferior resources. They think in a very practical way, and, like the Gnomes, are not too concerned with feelings if those get in the way of achieving a goal.

SORCERERS

In the center of the world lies the "Land of the Sorcerers." The inhabitants are people who are pretty comfortable in any of the other environments as they find it easy to adapt to change, so they frequently move in and out of the lands of their neighbors. They spend much of their time as diplomats and ambassadors, and some of them become great leaders. This stems from their ability to find ways of reconciling opposing viewpoints and overcoming barriers in order to move projects forward. Because the Sorcerers can easily change their behavior and appearance to fit the environment in which they find themselves, inhabitants from the other lands sometimes think they have magic powers, especially when they seem to be able to make others do whatever they have in mind, without question. However, their secret is their knowledge of the lands around them and the convincing way they can assimilate the behavior and language of their neighbors with chameleon-like ease.

So what on earth has all that got to do with optimum risk management? Well, it is a way of highlighting the people implications of risk taking in business. The intuitive and imaginative characteristics usually prevalent in entrepreneurial thinking need to be balanced by the pragmatic realism of those who have a genuine and justifiable concern for the stability and continuity of the enterprise. Too often one or the other is insufficiently prevalent, and some brilliant potential venture or product fails to materialize. The people with the various strengths need to be working as a team, with mutual respect and a leader who knows how to generate empathy in all of them towards the concerns and viewpoints of their colleagues. They are all valuable and necessary in a business which intends to adapt to trends and maintain a presence in its marketplace.

One thing which sets entrepreneurs apart from the average is their willingness to take risks in pursuit of the next exciting possibility. So it would seem natural to align entrepreneurship with risk taking. Every company has to embrace the idea of risk taking otherwise their product or service, sooner or later, becomes vulnerable to changes in market trends and customer expectations. The demand may not even necessarily be for a new product but maybe just for a different way of presenting a perfectly good one. Something as simple as the boredom factor or the competition will tempt a faithful consumer to try an alternative, but, whatever the reason for considering changes, a necessary ingredient is creativity. Innovation and creativity go hand in hand, and these are the notable features of the entrepreneurial mindset. What has to be considered, though, is at what stage of a company's development can the entrepreneur continue to take risks without serious consideration of the effects on other people and parts of the business?

You will remember from the traveler's tale, "The World of Business," entrepreneurs are the Explorers who want to keep on having new experiences and who can see possibilities, especially before the Gnomes. The Gnomes, of course, are the ones who are likely to be very averse to risk taking and want all kind of reassurances before putting their precious resources into some unproven venture. So what is the answer?

Maybe we should return to Ben Heirs and his decision thinking advice that advocates group thinking. Some might say that this means having lots of meetings to discuss the implications. The danger of this is that the Explorer and the Gnome in the business might end up at loggerheads with each other, or the Explorer would become so bored with the process that the initial excitement would wane. An opportunity would then be lost because some other idea would probably have replaced it in the Explorer's

mind, and, even worse, the communication gap would be widened. Much better, when the need arises, to formulate a well-balanced *prototype team,* drawn from all parts of the business, which could be given the task of taking the idea forward. They would be specially selected for their:
- Preferred thinking style
- Particular expertise and knowledge
- Style of operating in a team

They would not be a permanent fixture but would be people who have very current and practical experience of the departments they represent and who, at the end of a particular project, would return full-time to that department. This would not preclude them from future involvement in another prototype team, but the important point is that these teams should not become inhabitants of any kind of ivory tower or be perceived as such by the rest of the organization. Essentially, this kind of activity is, and should be, pragmatic in its purpose which is to keep the business where it wants and needs to be in the marketplace.

The selection process could involve the use of the Brain Technologies BrainMap Instrument together with the Belbin Team Styles Inventory in order to achieve the correct balance of thinking and behavior for each part of the process. This would be followed with some briefing workshops to ensure that every member of this newly formed group fully understands the requirements and terms of reference for the project, as well as the importance of the part each would play. The process would be cyclical, and its starting point would be the delegation to the participants of the task. They would be given the authority to take the original concept through all the stages of *exploration, analysis, experimentation, costing, testing, improving, reporting, and recommendation.* Their opinion as to feasibility or otherwise would be the basis of this recommendation to the board who would make the final decision. The strength of that decision, however, would be the availability of objective data gathered during the whole process as opposed to subjective opinions based on personal bias. Both the original Explorer and the Gnome would be available for consultation at any stage, and the team would have freedom to try things outside the norm, as well as the resources needed to carry out the task thoroughly. They would also be rewarded by recognition if the outcomes of their efforts prove beneficial to the company.

One reason why innovation teams fail is that companies frequently attempt similar approaches but do not recognize the need for the full commitment of the key resources—that is, time, release from other commitments, working space, and freedom to experiment, as well as the energizing activity of celebrating successes. In these circumstances, *Gnome-think* rules. Gnomes think in facts, numbers, words, and measurable results. But how do you measure the effort people will be prepared to put in simply because they feel enormous pride in something they have achieved for a company that does not take their input for granted but finds very public ways of showing gratitude? Explorers do lots of their thinking in pictures and feelings, and even words are most powerful when they are spoken with feeling. Imagining the benefits of a successful new product and anticipating the subsequent admiration by colleagues of those involved in bringing it to fruition is highly motivational. Enthusiasm can wane, however, if the preparation has been insufficient or unrealistic. Any exceptionally innovative experiment is almost guaranteed to encounter complexities along the way, so the team's energies must be conserved to deal with these, rather than distractions caused by demands on their attention that could have been avoided if appropriate preparatory thought had been given.

In order to diminish the likelihood of failure and eliminate the barriers to the team's progress, time needs to be spent before the onset in formulating a project proposal. This would realistically identify the level of involvement for each of the team members, together with the time frame at different stages. It will not necessarily be identical for each because of the nature of their differing contributions, so this has to be discussed and agreed at the outset. What would also be acknowledged would be the likely rewards according to the degree of success, thereby creating additional incentives. Some people would be pleased to be taking part just for the interest and novelty of some time spent in experimentation; for others it might be the prospect of some more tangible reward, maybe financial or developmental. The project proposal should be prepared by a Sorcerer who has the ability to comprehend the mindset of all of those who need to be supportive of the initiative and can take their potential objections into consideration. These would be anticipated and catered to and thereby would increase the likelihood of gaining general approval.

The key factor is the significance of balancing the need for innovation with the importance of not putting the stability of the organization at risk. In other words, *optimum risk management*. The risks involved in experimentation, with new products or system development, may in fact be considerably smaller than the risk of becoming complacent, either about ongoing demand or the methods of operation. The manager who knows what's going on, as I said earlier, is alert to both possibilities and knows when to respond accordingly. The following simple example of an outline proposal may be helpful.

PROJECT PROPOSAL

PROPOSER: John S.

SUBJECT: Review of warehouse operation

REASON FOR PROPOSING PROJECT:
It has been recognized for some time that there is an urgent need to improve and expand the operating system, and I now consider that this needs to be addressed, as a matter of urgency, for reasons of cost effectiveness. There is also the significance of the implications of our increased exporting activities.

Currently, the supervisory team is being strengthened, and new positions are being created. This suggests that it is appropriate to develop these new positions within the framework of an updated operation.

I am submitting this formal request to discuss in detail the terms of reference and authority to commence a project.

PROJECT OBJECTIVES:
1.   To devise methods which improve productivity through increased efficiency
2.   To reduce wastage and associated costs
3.   To formulate a method of operating which meets all requirements for quality assurance
4.   To expand the system so as to incorporate the activities relating to the special needs of exporting
5.   To recommend a system which will make optimum use of technological resources available to us
6.   To create a set of working practices which enhance staff job satisfaction levels resulting in improved morale

DEPARTMENTS INVOLVED:

Wa rehouse	Quality Assurance	Pattern Book Production
Laboratory	Stock Control	Telesales/Customer Service
Accounts	Data Processing	

SOURCES OF DIRECTION (Information and Resources):
James M.   Distribution Director

| Duncan R | Sales Director. |
| Robert L. | Financial Director |

TASK GROUP:

| John S. | Graham W. | Karen P. | Gary B. |
| George N. | Alison R. | Nita F. | Terry P. |

FACILITATOR: Anne M.   Training Manager

NATURE OF TASK (Terms of Reference):

1. Diagnostic:	Exploratory discussions on system needs and current inadequacies
2. Summarizing:	Agreements on beneficial changes
3. Action Plan:	Consensus on change implementation proposition
4. Budget:	Formulation of feasible schedule of costs
5. Implementation:	Recommendations for improvements and proposed timescale
6. Monitoring:	Schedule of dates for:

- Commencement of new system (or pilot)
- System monitoring
- Progress reviews

7. Reporting:	Proposal of final recommendations to directors (presentation)
8. Application:	Following acceptance of recommendations, immediate implementation of new system
9. Evaluation:	Regular monitoring of new system for ongoing improvement

PROPOSED PROJECT STARTING DATE:

TIME ALLOCATION FOR TASK GROUP:

John S. would coordinate and lead the project. There would probably be a time commitment of a varying nature during the life of the project, with a greater requirement at the beginning and end and with small segments of time from the group during the middle period. For example:

First Month	Approximately twenty-four hours (a half-day followed by twenty regular meetings of around two hours' duration)
Middle Period	One meeting per week
Final Month	As first month

Note: These are estimated times and may be adjusted.

PROPOSED COMPLETION DATE:

TERMS OF REFERENCE REQUIRED FROM DIRECTORS TO INCLUDE:
- What the project has to achieve
- Policy on all key issues
- The parameters of the project
- The limits of authority of the project team
- A target date for project report
- The project team members
- A starting date for the project
- An indication of support and commitment to the project from the board

One of the most obvious sources of information to project teams when they are charged with the task of improving systems is any group of people who are directly affected by the outputs. Two groups who are not consulted often enough but who are probably most affected are customers and suppliers. Both of these have very direct experience of the strengths and weaknesses in the actual operation of a company, but there is little evidence of truly effective approaches to obtaining this kind of insight. Too many companies rely on written questionnaires sent on a routine basis, with no real appreciation of the fact that busy people are not necessarily prepared to make the time to complete and return them.

Something as simple as actually engaging some of them in conversations on the subject can produce some amazing results. In a book that I read many years ago, *Up the Organization,* the author Robert Townsend says, "If all else fails, try honesty." This applies to so many things in business, but in trying to be slick, clever, and trendy something as simple as truth can so easily be lost. What is wrong with actually going to see your customers with the specific purpose of finding out how happy they are with what you are offering them and if that is the very best you could do for them? They will be delighted to tell you, and all you then have to do is go back to one of your prototype teams and ask them to work on making it a reality.

Attila the Hun once said, "Every decision involves some risk," but he also said, "It is unfortunate when final decisions are made by chieftains headquartered miles away from the front, where they can only guess at conditions and potentialities known only to the captain on the battlefield." Important strategic decisions in business should always only be made with the benefit of information and opinions garnered from the people at the "sharp end." Not only will they have the most up-to-date information on current trends and needs, it usually costs nothing to obtain this. You only have to ask! Whether it is a system, a product, or a service, they are the people who are affected by it, and they will be only too delighted to tell you how it could be bettered.

One of the most rewarding assignments I was ever engaged in was when I had been warning my client that I was concerned about the long-term viability of their product range. Their business was in the field of electronic engineering, supplying control systems to major industries. They were held in high esteem by their customers and felt very comfortable about the future demand for the products involved. Eventually they agreed that their key customers should be asked about their perceptions of their future needs and the likelihood of my client's products continuing to meet them. The approach taken was very carefully prepared and involved obtaining their willingness to take part in fairly lengthy interviews with myself. Although they were keen to express their sense of loyalty and admiration for my client, together with their hopes that they could continue to do business with them, they did admit to real concerns about the technological challenges they themselves were facing and the possibility that the current product range would be inadequate. They gladly disclosed what they perceived my client should be exploring and developing, and it is true to say that, at the time in question, that kind of research and development was not taking place. That information was priceless and directly resulted in an acknowledgement that if the appropriate investment in developing new products was not made, the company would be in danger of losing these key customers with the resulting implications for its future. They had been focusing on increasing their sales and finding new customers at the expense of the relationships that had provided them with millions of dollars worth of business for many years. So instead of increasing their sales force with the inevitable expenditure, they provided their engineers with the resources they needed to get into the exciting activity they loved of testing their own ingenuity and sense of achievement. The increase in their morale was enormous.

Optimum risk management involves investing some time in planning, but as the Scottish poet Robert Burns commented, "The best laid schemes o' mice and men gang aft agley," or to translate, "The best laid plans often go off the straight." However, Dwight D. Eisenhower said, "Plans are nothing—planning is everything." I say it's the thinking that really counts—and the collective thinking at that!

CHAPTER 6

Tenet Number 6—Shared Values

"A society is not really a society unless it is able to invent ideal concepts and myths that mobilise individual energies and bind people's souls together."

Pierre Thuillier

There are a number of ways in which it is possible to gain insight into a person's values, and one of the most visible of these is the way he or she behaves in relationships with others. This is equally true of organizations, and this is well known within those companies who have stayed in business for a number of generations. The significance of building and maintaining mutually beneficial relationships is appreciated by those who have managed to maintain successful organizations for many years and through economic variations world wide.

One of the key issues in the world of business today is the impact of technology on the way we all work. How many of the founders of the world's oldest companies would recognize their organizations today? Would they be delighted or horrified if they were looking down at their creations? Is there much difference between the old "satanic mills" of the nineteenth century where people were extensions of textile machinery and the modern open-plan offices where people are extensions of their computers?

Would those early founders embrace e-mail or voice mail as godsends? Would they accept voice mail or recorded telephone instructions as adequate ways of communicating with customers whose loyalty they wish to maintain? And what about keeping people holding on the phone for the personal touch, while canned music dribbles on? In short, is technology all useful wizardry or a blight on all human contact?

Companies who ask themselves these questions and then try to find a balanced way of making optimum use of technology, without losing the major benefits of human interaction, will be the leaders in tomorrow's world.

In 1995 Charles Handy, one of the highly respected observers of our time, delivered a lecture to the RSA (The Royal Society for the encouragement of the Arts, Manufactures, and Commerce) which stimulated much discussion about the future of British business and the competitiveness of UK companies in the global business environment. This resulted in the RSA commissioning a business-led inquiry which revealed some very profound findings in relation to common factors apparent in those companies world wide who had a long-standing record of success and were admired as "world class" organizations. Those common factors were invariably linked to strong identities derived from the values and philosophy of the organization and a commitment to constant attention to the key relationships with others who could and did have an impact on the company's operation. These were:

- Customers
- Suppliers
- Employees
- Shareholders
- The Community at Large

It was recognized that the concentrated focus on the "bottom line," often at the expense of things that affected the company's reputation in a major way, did not necessarily lead to long-term success and profitability.

How can you be getting the best for your business if some of the most important relationships that have a significant impact on your results are unsatisfactory on either side? When the chips are down and things are difficult, it is often your relationship history that makes the difference between getting that bit of extra cooperation you need and not getting it. But it is more than that. It goes deeper. We need a wider intelligence for operating on a global basis, as much because of the cultural differences in approaches to doing business as the actual issues of competition. So there is the values dimension. My early experience of working in a small stockbroking office in Glasgow taught me about how people respond to integrity and mutual respect.

I was appalled when I moved to the Midlands of England and saw people get up from their desks, put on their coats, and stand waiting for a bell to ring so that they could rush out of the building at five o'clock. They did not feel part of anything in that company. In Glasgow, I had frequently worked very late because there were important things to be finished, but I *knew* that my boss actually cared about my future, and we *all* cared about how we did things for our customers. As well as that, we all had a profit-sharing bonus and periodic first-class social events paid for by the company. There was a sense of "fair play" and of being part of a quality team which made me incredibly proud and loyal about working for Mr. Paul. He was a man of integrity who traveled the world looking at the operation of the companies he was advising people to invest in, so the business came because people trusted him and the people he chose to work with him. I will always be profoundly grateful for the influence that man had on my life because I was fortunate enough to have my first experience of being employed in his company.

Those kinds of values seemed to disappear in the nineteen-eighties, and as a country the British began to operate in a culture of "screw everybody else and get what you can" across the whole spectrum of society. Put that together with the short-term requirements of the banking fraternity and the mischief making of many in the media, and all you have is a recipe for cynicism and despair.

Fortunately, what came out of the initiative sparked off by Charles Handy's comments was that a number of high-profile businesspeople in the country began to say that there has to be a better way and started to support and advocate the "inclusive approach" and reduce the over-reliance on financial measures of performance.

The movement which emerged after the findings of the original RSA report is "The Centre for Tomorrow's Company." This is dedicated to inspiring and enabling businesses to adopt the inclusive approach as a means of "achieving sustainable success linked with the pursuit of long-term goals in a manner consistent with a company's core purpose and core values." All of the research that they have commissioned or carried out verifies their claims that the values espoused by an organization have a direct effect on the perceptions that their stakeholders have of them and ultimately of the loyalty and commitment that this generates.

My own theory is that a company is an entity that is surrounded by an aura, the nature of which is directly attributable to the ethics and standards by which it operates. This affects its every business activity and interaction. Having entered hundreds of business establishments throughout my career, I invariably have a sense of the prevailing environment of each one almost immediately. There are always indicators of how the people in the company relate to visitors as well as each other, and these are signaled in all kinds of ways. How much attention has been paid to the convenience and comfort of people who are unfamiliar with the establishment? Can they park their cars without too much hassle? If they have to wait, is the reception staff friendly and helpful? Is there an acknowledgement that their time is valuable and an effort made to ensure that they are not kept waiting longer than is courteous? Are the company people smiling and friendly to each other? Is the reception area open, bright, and clean? Is there up-to-date reading material if no one is engaging them in conversation? When leaving, are they escorted to the door rather than left to find their own way through a maze of corridors? In other words, do they have the feeling that they are important?

All stakeholders in a business have expectations as to how they should be treated. We all know that shareholders, quite rightly, expect to have a satisfactory financial return on their investment. But what about the others? What do they expect and hope for?

CUSTOMERS: They will expect to be provided with products and services within the parameters of what is known as the "seven rights."

- **Right Product**
- **Right Price**
- **Right Place**
- **Right Time**
- **Right Quality**
- **Right Service**
- **Right Attitude**

STAFF: They will hope to experience stability of employment in an organization which values their contribution and enables them to demonstrate their worth both as employees and members of society.

SUPPLIERS: They will want to serve an organization which shows integrity within their business relationship and recognizes their need to survive into the future by respecting the contractual accountability on both sides.

COMMUNITY: Those who share their location will expect recognition of the impact which a business operation has upon the economy, environment, and social well-being of the other inhabitants, whether this be in a local context or globally.

To some extent, this falls into the category of leadership, also. Groups or individuals who play some significant role in any community are liable to become role models for others, whether or not they intend or wish to. In that sense, they attain some kind of responsibility for setting a good example to others, and they ignore it at their peril. There have been examples of very large multinational companies who have felt themselves to be impervious to criticism who have suddenly felt the weight of public disapproval and its immediate effect on their bottom line. They have then been forced to take immediate steps to alter their perceived unethical stance. What was highlighted, however, was the fact that the values of the community at large were not those of the organization, and as a result the customers abandoned their loyalty and took their business elsewhere.

The same trait occurs internally within companies, and the successful entrepreneur, instinctively or deliberately, cultivates a climate of participation which is based on common awareness of "doing the right thing." To a great extent, values and ethics are more about what we will *not* do to promote our business interests rather than what we will do. The things we *can* do are multitudinous, so we have many choices. But in the ethical business the people know when they would be getting down in the mud, and they spontaneously act within a relatively small number of constraints which company policy clearly indicates. They know the things which would tarnish the company's reputation because the behavior and standards which operate naturally on a daily basis demonstrate "the way we do things round here." When they are comfortable with that, they have the sense of being part of something that embodies their own values. When they are not comfortable, they will feel alienated and uncertain about how they should proceed. Uncertainty breeds misunderstanding, and misunderstanding creates delay as well as the possibility of making wrong decisions.

Any person who has started his or her own business from scratch and experienced all the anxieties involved in taking it forward will also have learned the importance of the preservation of human dignity, being able to trust in the promises that others make, and the agony of being on the receiving end of dishonest practices that could result in the loss of all that they have struggled for. This is why the ultimately, truly successful ones remember these feelings and communicate their abhorrence of company practices that offend the dignity of others or take unfair advantage of the people who believe in the integrity of their company's products, services, and relationships. There is an old adage in the sales profession which says, "People don't buy products, they buy happiness," and Mark McCormack in his book *What They Don't Teach You at Harvard Business School* says, "All things being equal, people like to do business with a friend—all things not being equal, people still like to do business with a friend." How long does a friendship last if one of the parties involved is regularly taking advantage of the other? Friends may forgive one instance of disappointment in the actions which have disadvantaged them, but it is unlikely that they will continue allowing their associate to insult their intelligence and betray their trust. No one enjoys the pain of being let down, and insightful businesspeople know that this applies to all of their stakeholders.

We should not ignore the importance of this message when we are operating globally. If we intend to do business with people from countries whose cultures are different from our own, it is imperative that we take the trouble not to offend their dignity or that of their laws or religions. Some of the things we take for granted as being generally acceptable can be unforgivable for them. I once heard a story of the captain who was chased around his own ship by a cook whom he had reprimanded in front of his peers. In that man's culture, this was a complete loss of face, and he had nothing now to lose by attacking his employer. The captain should have known that human dignity was paramount in that employee's native land and a public reprimand was, for him, beyond the pale. If this is the effect on an employee, what would be the impact if we were to make similar mistakes with potential customers or suppliers? It goes without saying that anyone aspiring to do business abroad will almost certainly find it extremely difficult if they do not take the trouble to learn about the value systems of the foreign cultures they will encounter.

One of the most fascinating and informative books on this subject is *The Seven Cultures of Capitalism* by Charles Hampden-Turner and Alfons Trompenaars. They studied the unique cultural habits and traditions of the United States, Britain, France, Germany, Japan, Sweden, and the Netherlands, and this should probably be compulsory reading for anyone considering becoming involved in strategic alliances with operators from any of these countries or the setting up of branches which would be run along the same lines as those in their home country. A number of very successful UK businesses have discovered this too late, to their cost. What the book does not deal with, of course, is all of the other countries in the world who have emerged as major players, either as competitors, potential workforce, or an enormous new customer base. As far as Europe is concerned, John Mole's *Mind Your Manners* is an excellent source of tips to avoid culture clashes. But what about the rest of the world? What do our entrepreneurs have to learn about the norms in other continents? What are the protocols involved in dealing with the Chinese? What are the habits that Arabs find disgusting? How do Indians expect their managers to behave? For which countries do our entrepreneurs need to have extremely watertight financial arrangements if they are to ensure receipt of payments for their goods?

The phenomenon of the Internet has completely changed the parameters of business operation very rapidly, but deeply held convictions and values of people will take much longer to integrate even if the desire is strong. That is not to say that we should not endeavor to constantly increase mutual respect and understanding, although we should be realistic enough to acknowledge that it will take time and effort. But the company that intends to stay around will make the effort and invest the time because they know that the payback will be enormous.

The new world of business raises many challenges, not the least of which is the increasing shortage of executives either willing or able to meet these. Within the US corporate sector, research has identified that 40 percent of newly hired executives fail within the first eighteen months, and two out of every five newly recruited managers don't last beyond the first year and a half. There is, I believe, a values dimension to this. The majority of these corporate giants are stuck in a rut of old paradigms about the ways businesses should function and what people expect from them, both investors and employees. What is happening is that many of the best young potential executives are opting to work in the more exciting and rewarding environment of the small and medium-sized enterprises, and, increasingly, investors too are attracted to the more entrepreneurial cultures inherent in these companies where the need to be innovative is more pressing in order to survive.

There are a number of significant behaviors and attitudes that this engenders and which very large organizations find difficult or even impossible to sustain. These include:

Adaptability	Small companies need people to be adaptable because they cannot afford too many specialists. In order to have sufficient "job cover," people have to learn about each other's jobs and help out in times of absence or emergency. In particular, executives have to perform functions for which large organizations would employ professionals.
Creativity	Small companies find it difficult to acquire the resources they need because of shortage of funds, so they have to find alternative approaches to running certain aspects of their businesses so as to minimize expenditure.
Coaching	External training is often not an option for small companies, again because of cost constraints, so there is much reliance on in-house knowledge and skills transfer. It may not always be of the quality which purist trainers would advocate, but it does have to be sufficient for the learners to acquire a degree of competence so that the tasks in question can be carried out.
Knowledge Creation and Learning	As a result of the three issues mentioned above, new knowledge is created internally. The degree of sharing of information that takes place in those circumstances cannot be avoided. The proximity with which people have to operate together produces an enforced environment of openness. The opportunities for hoarding information or hiding failures are substantially less than in larger, more compartmentalized establishments.
Team Building	Any of the behaviors and attitudes which large companies have to initiate through training activities happen more naturally in small companies where people have to learn to cooperate with each other out of necessity. The shared need to survive means that, for them, there is no requirement to create imaginary scenarios in training courses. They live with such situations every day.
Shared Destinies	Individuals working in small companies are much more vulnerable to the consequences of company failure. There is less likelihood of compensations if redundancies become inevitable, so they must pull together to make things work and enhance their own futures.

SHARED VALUES

A common factor which runs through all of the above is the emotional implication. This is a mixture of the inevitability of those involved to manage the closeness of their relationships and the passion frequently felt by those owners who have started the business from scratch. The struggles involved in building a new business are not dissimilar to those experienced by parents of a growing family, and the passionate determination to make it succeed is why so many refer to their business as "my baby." They often have difficulty in letting it go when it starts to grow into something very different from the enterprise they have nurtured through all kinds of testing obstacles, and the people who have shared the experience with them have an attachment which even they cannot always explain. These entrepreneurial owners frequently display the same qualities as those we choose to refer to as charismatic. They appear to have some mysterious energy which almost hypnotizes people into doing what we refer to as "going the extra mile." Those same people often wonder themselves why they do it, especially when the charismatic person is also unpredictable and prone to bouts of prima donna type of behavior.

When the business has reached the stage of growth at which it can no longer be maintained by the owners calling on the personal loyalties of each of the employees to meet extraordinary demands, it is time to change the manner in which it operates. This is why, in the event of the charismatic entrepreneur staying in the leadership role, the organization can start to become out of control. The needs of the business often become secondary to the old loyalties, and either the leader does not recognize this or is "in denial" even when it is apparent that some decisions have been proved inappropriate and made for the wrong reasons. The time has come for the style of leadership to change and the role of chief executive to move into the hands of one who is less emotionally attached. This is also the time for serious consideration of the implications of such a change.

The problem with charismatic leaders is that when they leave there is an enormous feeling of having been deserted amongst many of the organization's people. If this is not taken sufficiently seriously, many of those who have been instrumental in the success up to that point will be the ones who feel aggrieved, with all of the emotional baggage that this entails. One of the secrets of managing this situation is to look closely at the values which have been integral to the company's operation from the start and to endeavor to maintain the best of them whilst introducing the new processes necessary to manage the future development of the business. If this can be achieved, then people will be less likely to feel bereft at the loss of the old regime and more reassured about the possibilities ahead.

The expectations that people have in organizations have a direct correlation to the culture that has grown within it. To try to change these rapidly or insensitively is folly indeed. The wise new leader is the one who takes this challenge as seriously as any of the other less emotionally charged policy decisions involved in the way forward and makes "informed" plans to meet it.

The topic of charisma is explored further in the following chapter.

CHAPTER 7

Tenet Number 7—Morale Maintenance

"Thoughts are associated in the mind not just by content but by mood. People have what amounts to a set of bad-mood thoughts that come to mind more readily when they are feeling down...depressed people seem to use one depressing topic to get their minds off another, which only stirs more negative emotions."

Emotional Intelligence, by Daniel Goleman

There is nothing more likely to drain people's energy than depression stemming from ongoing feelings of insecurity, and if there is one thing we cannot avoid in the workplace today it is the absence of certainty. The days have gone when we could take our customers or even our marketplace for granted. Competition can come from the most unlikely directions at any time, and whilst we must maintain our alertness to this, we must not cultivate feelings of fear about it. In her book *Leading from the Heart*, Kay Gilley comments, "Acknowledging fear allows us to examine possible outcomes and discuss how we can turn each scenario into a winning situation. When we are able to accept the worst case scenario, we develop new confidence that whatever outcome develops, both we and our organization will benefit from it." Good leaders instinctively know that people perform best when they have a positive mindset and an expectation of opportunities and alternatives, so an important task is to maintain the morale of the group.

It has long been asserted that the best type of leadership emanates from very charismatic individuals, and there is no doubt that charisma is a major, if somewhat indefinable, advantage to those who possess it. But charisma, by itself, does not necessarily produce the best business results. If the charismatic leader also has an aptitude and ability to rationalize the implications of trends and options throughout the business scenario, then the likelihood of predictable success is multiplied. There are interesting examples of people who could recognize the kind of approach to business which would produce results in particular sets of circumstances mainly through the study of what was actually going on around them. Their approach to directing their business could better be described as thoughtful as opposed to intuitive, and this, of course, leads to the question of which is the most appropriate. Should you base leadership of your organization on facts, figures, structure, and systems, or on the excitement of visions of possibilities, belief in potential, unlimited horizons, and conviction that anything can be achieved through sheer determination?

My own conviction is that it is a mixture of both, and the best leaders know how to balance the application of each. When things are difficult and uncertain, people need to feel that they understand the realities of their situation, confident that the management team in their organization is able to respond to current circumstances in ways which have the best interests of the business at heart and that they act with integrity. When people have confidence in their leaders and those leaders respect the intelligence as well as the concerns of their people, the mutual trust involved will play a major part in the maintenance of morale even when things are very tough. Appealing to peoples' emotions to "stick it out" when they do not trust the information made available to them is more likely to produce cynicism and disrespect rather than motivation. However, if people can intuitively feel that the leader truly believes in the right way ahead and can give them credible reasons why, they are less likely to lose faith. They will believe that any extra effort needed will be rewarded, not only materially, but emotionally, in terms of the knowledge that their contribution has been accepted, recognized, and valued.

There is little long-term benefit in having a charismatic leader of an organization if that person allows fundamentally uncaring, self-seeking, and incompetent executives or managers to abuse the goodwill and efforts of the people in cynical ways. This is giving the lie to the promises and exhortations of the person at the top. In those circumstances, both the well-meaning leader and all of the other stakeholders in the business are being betrayed. It may not be fashionable to contend that good management is at the root of business success, but without it today's darlings of the stock market can often become tomorrow's has-beens.

Whether we talk about business, politics, or wars, the common factor in terms of the morale aspect of leadership is that of belief in the leader's personal commitment—the kind of commitment that is apparent on a day-to-day basis by the actual physical presence of the leader, being seen to participate in the reality of overcoming frustrations and obstacles. Engendering the feeling of "we're in this together" does not usually take place as a result of slogans on posters and periodic pep-talks, both of which very quickly lose their impact and just become part of the workplace clutter, either physical or verbal. Togetherness is much more likely to happen when leaders walk about in the working environment, asking people questions and actively listening to their responses. These might be opinions, concerns, ideas, suggestions, grumbles, requests for information, or simply progress reports and data. The thing that makes the difference is the fact that the person or people who make the influential decisions truly want to know what is going on in people's minds and, where necessary, take appropriate action. The number of enterprises or projects that have turned from success and promise into oblivion because of the gradual removal of the influential presence of senior management in the field of operation is legion.

Managerial style has a significant effect on the manner of an operation's performance, but the element which has the most crucial impact is the evidence of personal influence from the top on how things happen. How many times have you been impressed with an establishment and then, over time, have gradually begun to notice that little things are changing, including the people and the way in which they interact with you? Standards are beginning to slip, staff turnover seems constantly apparent, errors are taking place more frequently, and nobody is taking any interest in getting to know you or showing genuine concern over your levels of satisfaction. There may be the perfunctory question "is everything all right for you?" but there is no real eye contact when you reply and things are not so bad that you feel inclined to complain. It's just that the little details that make the difference are missing. You never see "management" around the place any more, and the whole atmosphere is different. If that depresses you and makes you feel less inclined to visit that establishment than you used to be, how do you think the people who work there are feeling? The enterprise is going backwards instead of forward, and you can all sense it.

Anyone who has heard of or read about the work of biologist Rupert Sheldrake, who postulated the existence of what was described as "*morphogenic fields,*" will appreciate the significance of *feeling* atmospheres within places. Whether you are visiting a place of business, someone's home, a place of entertainment, a church, or just an old building, you experience, to a greater or lesser extent, positive or negative feelings when you enter it, particularly on your first visit. Sheldrake and some others suggest that places have waves of energy which spread out within the space of the regions of inhabited places, and these waves are created by the behaviors of the people who occupy them and the messages that those behaviors send out. Those who have studied and written about "*field theory*" and the behavior of matter as particles have stimulated research into the provocative possibilities of fields of energy within organizational space. The concept is fascinating in its implications, and those of us who in this respect are "laypeople" can only ask ourselves if the feelings we experience when we first enter a place and immediately decide whether we like it or not have those feelings reinforced later by what we observe and experience as time goes on.

It cannot be denied that the mood of employees is communicated in all kinds of ways that contribute to the prevailing environment of an organization. Moods are contagious, and positive energy created by high spirits tends to create positive responses from those touched by it, and this, in turn, increases the volume generated. The same, of course, applies in the opposite circumstances, and then negativity prevails. When we are willing to acknowledge that we can really affect each other's moods, then we might also consider the likelihood of symbiosis between leaders and those who are their followers. This symbiosis, or state of mutual dependency, is the generally unacknowledged phenomenon that reinforces the exchange of energy between us. People "pick up" the energy of their leaders when in contact with them, and simultaneously the leaders are encouraged or disappointed by the behavior of their people. Encouragement stimulates positive reactions, these transmit positive signals, and the exchange energizes both.

Morale maintenance emanates more from unspoken positive messages transmitted through spontaneous behavior than from deliberately constructed speeches. The old adage that "actions speak louder than words" truly applies in this sense because, in organizations, people make judgments based on the long-term, consistent types of action and attitudes. These are the indicators that count, not the trendy "flavor of the month" initiatives which inevitably fail because they are imported and not generated from the very heart of the business. Morale maintenance is a mutual responsibility and a shared commodity. Leaders who assume total responsibility for this are naïve, and followers who assume no responsibility for it are immature. The resulting relationship is that of *Parent/Child*, and our new world of business will only tolerate intelligent *Adult* relationships in which sharing of responsibility for outcomes and results is both accepted and apparent. There is, however, another old adage which says "all work and no play makes Jack a dull boy," and it cannot be denied that one of the features of today's world of work for many people is the high level of stress induced by increasingly long hours spent at work. Technology has replaced human beings in thousands of jobs, but the saving in manpower has brought its own high cost in other forms. As yet, much of the technology is far from perfect in terms of its reliability, and, when it fails to perform, not only massive amounts of time are lost, frustration levels experienced by both staff and customers are massively high. Frustration saps energy as well as patience, and the effort required from staff to maintain professionalism on these occasions is enormous. One of the best stress management techniques available to us all is laughter between friends, and if this is common in the workplace it relieves tensions, and it is usually an indicator of good morale.

I have memories of spending a considerable amount of time in a client company who took great pride in their professionalism, and I regarded them very highly for this. I could not fail to notice, however, that in spite of the extremely high numbers of people in the huge open-plan offices, the atmosphere was always surprisingly quiet and subdued. People did not leave their unusually tidy desks very often, and the only laughter I used to encounter would be from the delegates when they were in the training room with my colleagues and myself. When we eventually discreetly commented on this, we found out that people were fundamentally unhappy working for the company but stayed because the salaries and other benefits were comparatively good. Those delegates who came from other regions of the same company were often heard to comment on the difference they also noticed in the attitudes of their head office opposite numbers. When listening to the way each of the two groups talked of their feelings about the company, it was difficult to believe that they worked for the same organization. Those from some regional offices were highly motivated, cheerful, and very willing to learn and participate, whilst the head office group were cynical and mainly interested in describing how bad their managers were or what could be obtained from the training which would help them to improve their resumes. The other noticeable factor was that the happy group displayed loyalty and playfulness towards one another and were proud of the length of time they had been working colleagues. I was also aware of the fact that their regional results were of a very high order. There was no doubt that they had fun, but they were an excellent team. It was also interesting to note that the managers of the happy groups had previously enrolled in the pilot courses of the training program and showed interest in their people's ideas for implementing developmental follow-up.

There are advocates of fun in the workplace who believe that it can be created by specially designed activities whose objectives are to improve working relationships, and to a degree it can happen. But it is my contention that the fun is more likely to be the outcome of working groups caring enough about helping each other to succeed, and in the process obtaining strong feelings of security about the value of their collective achievement. This means that their energies are focused on their shared working objectives as opposed to unhealthy mistrust and competition with each other. They trust each other enough to laugh together, and the true measure is when their managers are part of the jocularity and not the butt of it!

If you want to judge the morale of your organization, look at the following:
- How much absenteeism occurs?
- Do people exchange jokes as opposed to sarcastic comments?
- Do people help each other to solve problems?
- Is the management team respected as opposed to tolerated?
- Do people feel informed?
- Are people willing to put forward ideas and opinions?
- Are people concerned about maintaining standards?
- Are mistakes used to increase learning as opposed to allocating blame?
- Is there a culture of results achievement?
- Do people enjoy occasionally socializing together?
- Does the group celebrate success?
- **DO YOU ENJOY GOING TO WORK?**

If the answers are mainly positive, then morale is probably being well maintained.

CHAPTER 8

Tenet Number 8—Culture of Participation

"Wherever men or groups think of themselves not only as responsible for their own work, but sharing in a responsibility for the whole enterprise, there is a much greater chance of success for that enterprise."

Essays on Management, by Mary Parker Follett

When Mary Parker Follett made that statement in the 1920s, the world of work was very different from that of today, but the wisdom of the sentiment is, I believe, even more relevant to today's society than she could have known. The philosophy behind this book is that some fundamentals concerning people and their responses to work as part of their lives do not change. The feelings of self-worth that people experience when the effort they put into the work they do is valuable, and perceived as such by others, have an immense effect on the levels of energy they can and will continue to invest in the organization that employs them.

The *Oxford Dictionary* defines "to participate" as "*to have share in,*" but recent interpretations of having share in, within the context of the workplace, unfortunately have been in many instances limited to considerations of power over others and material reward. The real root of work-related satisfaction is more primeval than is generally recognized. Why else will many people continue to work in professions which are of immense help to society such as nursing or firefighting when the material rewards are so much less than the value of the contribution they make? How well is this considered by the leaders of more mundane occupations?

In his book *Further up the Organisation*, Robert Townsend comments, "Organisations work when they maximise the chance that each one, working with others, will get for growth in his job. You can't motivate people. That door is locked from the inside. You **can** create a climate in which most people will motivate themselves to help the company reach its objectives. Like it or not, the only practical act is to adopt participative-management assumptions and get going." Townsend, of course, was not an academic theorist. He was speaking as a highly recognized and pragmatic achiever of business success through insight and observation, obtained during a distinguished business career, often managing unmanageable situations.

The mistake that many managers make is in not learning to understand the difference between incentives and motivation. All of the incentives in the world will have limited effect in the longer term if the climate is one of tight control from the top. The turnover of bright young management trainees in some large organizations has a direct relationship with the degree to which they experience opportunities to express their ideas or creativity. The cost to the companies they desert goes far beyond the financial one of salaries and training that has been invested in them up to the time of their exit. The enthusiasm, energy, and freshness which made them appealing in the first place is gradually stifled, resulting in feelings of frustration, boredom, and finally disillusionment. This is the point at which the best of them decide to move on and find occupations that offer them more challenge, enjoyment, and a sense of achievement. Even at the expense of highly attractive salaries and other benefits, such as incentives, they prefer to go where they can feel emotionally rewarded, that is, motivated. The incentives are external and controllable by the management, but the motivation is internal, so is not readily available for manipulation. The problem for the organizations that these bright young people leave is that it is often many years before the effect of the paucity of fresh ideas and creativity is reflected in the company performance levels. The larger the organization, the longer it can continue to live off its reputation and ignore the signals that indicate that, like the Titanic, it is heading for disaster. When the decline is finally apparent, it is enormously difficult to "turn the ship around."

There is a need, however, to define what is really indicative of true participation in the company sense. Let us start with the word *participate* as defined by the *Oxford Dictionary*, that is, *have share in*. If we further explore the word *share*, it defines this as "portion detached for individual from common amount," and, "part one is entitled to have or bound to contribute." Unfortunately, our society today places most emphasis on the *entitlement* aspect and little emphasis on the *contribution* aspect, and this is what proves to be the stumbling block in the potential development of truly participative cultures in business.

If we refer back to transactional analysis and the concept of ego states as personality segments displaying particular behavioral patterns, we will remember that the three main ego states are *Parent, Adult,* and *Child.* Eric Berne postulated that each of us could stimulate, and be stimulated by, behavior and attitudes of others. This is just as apparent in working relationships as in any other, and the *Parent/Child* culture is the perfect example of a non-participative one. In this instance, whether the *Parent* is critical or nurturing, there is the acceptance on both sides that responsibility for decision making and ensuring of performance requirements lies with the management and not with the individual. This provokes what is cynically known as "mushroom management"—that is, "being kept in the dark and covered with fertilizer from a great height." In an *Adult/ Adult* relationship environment, the main feature is that of mutual respect for the each other's capability and acceptance of responsibility for negative aspects of business challenges as well as positive. There is, therefore, an open culture in which individuals feel informed and able to voice opinions as well as display competence and promote ideas. This engenders a feeling of having a degree of control of personal destiny and thereby the motivation to contribute to the betterment of the organization. Charles Handy commented, "It is immoral to steal people's responsibility," and I believe that this theft suppresses their adulthood.

If it is so simple, however, one could question why all companies do not adopt this operating style. The truth is that it is not easily applied overnight because of human nature itself and the individual upbringing, education, role models, and expectations that we all have. So it must be worked at, and trust as well as commitment must be nurtured on both sides. The biggest barrier to achieving a truly participative culture is that of fear. Some managers are afraid to trust people with information and responsibility, and some employees are unwilling to take responsibility for their own job security. The behaviors that each adopts in those circumstances reinforce the antipathy they both feel, and the old culture continues. Until and unless the most influential party, that is the leader, makes a determined and sustained effort to attract the trust of the followers, attempts at initiatives to change the working practices and communication style will tend to be short-term, "flavor of the month" occurrences. This scenario is most likely in larger organizations because even if the head of the company is determined, many middle managers, afraid of losing their own power base, will actively, or covertly, ensure that it does not happen. They will show tacit acceptance of the new policy, but they will not, in the relatively less public environment of their own sphere of influence, abandon their autocracy. Since the result of this is that their people inevitably continue to act in a compliant manner but without enthusiasm, the initiative becomes discredited and eventually fails.

In smaller companies, unhelpful behavior is more quickly observed, and a climate of real democracy, which is how I would describe the *Adult/Adult* relationship, can be sustained. In any good team, non-participators are soon ousted because their colleagues rapidly recognize that the kind of contribution they do make is counter-productive. In small working groups it is also more difficult to keep secret trends in the nature of the business and the way people perform within it, so people do know what is going on. The leaders then have the choice of acknowledging situations or of burying their heads in the sand and pretending that problems are not apparent to others. Practical heads of successful smaller organizations then instinctively cultivate open relationships knowing that to do otherwise would be pointless. This is why people who have spent the bulk of their working lives in smaller companies find it extremely difficult to accept the politics and power-play inherent in large organizations where "the grapevine" is the most commonly accepted channel of communication.

If there is a formula for the participative culture, it would most likely be a cyclical process which would involve an approach that I have described as *"Achievement Management Orientation (AMO)."* It is a rather unwieldy label, but as a concept it is a philosophy rather than a system, and it can be adapted to meet any company's situation. It is a method of management communication that I have designed after years of concentrated involvement with companies who were taking a determined approach to changing the way their organizations operated.

As I stated at the beginning of this book, I recognized that the formula for success was quite straightforward and based on ancient truths, but what was needed was an approach that could work in small and medium-sized organizations as well as large ones. The cornerstone elements are:

- Mutual respect in all interactions with colleagues, customers, and suppliers
- Acceptance of personal responsibility for all work activities with accountability to colleagues for contribution
- Exchange of thoughts and ideas on information, trends, and developments that affect the ongoing success of the organization and the future security of all stakeholders, that is, shareholders, employees, customers, and suppliers
- Ongoing attention to market information and recognition of necessary responses, involving all departments in the response decisions
- An internal communication structure which is understood by all and which touches every individual in the organization.

There is considerable emphasis on **market research and response**, **decision thinking involvement**, and **personal achievement recognition**, and I consider it to be an approach which appeals to the self-esteem and self-preservation emotions in people. This makes it, therefore, highly motivational when properly understood and applied. It is a very *Adult* approach to work interaction and assumes that people will prefer this to the previously more common *Parent/Child* relationship between "bosses" and "workers" described earlier in this chapter.

In order to maintain success in business, there is a need to ensure that the key functions within it work in conjunction with each other and not as separate and divisive operations. It is also necessary to ensure that these key functions are regularly monitored as to their impact and contribution:

- Market Research
- Sales Management
- Financial Planning
- Production Efficiency
- Customer Care
- People Development
- Communication

If they are perceived as separate functions of varying importance, divisive attitudes, empire building, and prima donna groups inevitably result in a reduction in co-operation. All the key functions are integral parts of the success formula, and, as such, deserve their rightful place in the monitoring agenda as well as the strategic planning process. As individuals and groups achieve the right results within those functions, the organization should applaud them.

Achievement Orientation is a positive approach at times of necessity for tangible results. It is particularly relevant when changes or pressures are likely to increase negative stress at all levels. If there is a general perception that security is threatened or failure to achieve objectives is deemed possible, people crave direction and good leadership. Absence of clear leadership at difficult times produces feelings of confusion or panic. So how does it work?

It is based on a clear definition and expression of the company's task requirement using measurable criteria for every department:
- Financial targets
- Practical activities of the work involved (tasks)
- Volume of work necessary
- Productivity aspects
- Cost maintenance
- Resources available and used

Who does what?
- Managers acquaint themselves thoroughly with the financial objectives of the organization.
- Managers ensure they have realistic and specific financial and/or practical performance targets **agreed upon** for their departments.
- Managers translate the financial targets into specific, practical task requirements for each person reporting to them and communicate, through exploratory two-way discussion, the implications and end results to be achieved.
- Teams jointly monitor achievements using data from the company management information system during achievement reviews—**at least monthly**.

Because of its clarity of purpose, *Achievement Management Orientation* will reinforce the leadership ethos and relegate financial control to its rightful function of being a key tool of management but not a panacea in itself. The desired results of business are expressed in financial terms, but the means of achieving a desired result is a fine mix of the charismatic ability to inspire together with a practical awareness and application of the realities involved. If ongoing success is to be the outcome of management activities, then the balance must be perceived and sustained.

This philosophy uses the same approach to data collection and application for information exchange as does the simply financial alternative, but the emphasis is laid on using job content criteria, rather than on financial criteria, for motivation at all levels. Managers must translate the desired financial results into job-specific achievement data to be used as the basis for "achievement reviewing," thus enabling people to relate their day-to-day activities to the financial contribution required. It is not the responsibility of the achievers to translate financial criteria into task objectives—that is the responsibility of the managers who should be sufficiently knowledgeable of financial systems and terminology to effect the transition. The clumsy imposition of financial management and technology which is not tempered by skilful leadership communication may produce compliance, but it will not produce excellence, innovation, or commitment. Three decades ago, compliance may have been sufficient for survival, and in some less developed economies may still be now, but in the much more competitive environment of this new century, adaptability is the commodity which shareholders will be buying when they invest. Adaptability is more likely to be obtained from people who are not afraid of change, and commitment is never a bedfellow of fear. There must, therefore, be a culture of team support with the managers being perceived as full members of the team. The role within the team that leaders/managers play involves them in displaying a number of abilities, skills, and knowledge which collectively earn them their credibility as key members, the ones who really bring out the best in others. These include:

- Ability to recognize business objectives expressed in financial terms
- Ability to relate financial objectives to group requirement and individual achievement contributions
- Ability to communicate the achievement contribution requirements in order to obtain accountability commitment, both team and individual
- Ability to agree upon appropriate control systems and data criteria for monitoring ongoing, day-to-day achievement of contribution
- Ability to translate achievement at occupational level back to the business objectives for purposes of recognition and re-motivation

These abilities will become enhanced as knowledge and skill increase through training and experience of certain management competencies:
- Financial planning and business control
- Devising co-ordinating objectives
- Achievement discussion (as opposed to assessment interviewing)
- Performance coaching
- Effective information exchange
- Decision thinking
- Monitoring and response to key data impacting on the business
- Task group application

Training people, particularly managers, to apply this philosophy is necessary to its success, and the first person to address is the chief executive who must **want it, understand it, believe in it, and must be personally committed to it.** Without these, it will fail. The chief executive is the chief coach and champion, and the managers are the leading players who maintain the vital team support culture.

The earlier reference to the cyclical nature of leading achievement involves a number of stages in "**The Achievement Cycle**," and each of these stages requires appropriate action. After identifying the current **key task** as the starting point, the stages illustrated in the following model are: ***Thinking, Deciding, Communicating, Delegating, and Monitoring.*** And these are always ended by celebrating success before starting the next new task. Celebration renews the spirit and creates energy for another challenge.

Every business is the equivalent of a small world which has its own characteristics but is inevitably affected by the other worlds which share its universe, so, as well as internal considerations, there are external factors which affect all decision making and practices. These various considerations influence and sometimes constrain the way the achievement cycle eventually operates, and I have labeled them "**Elements of Impact.**" The model illustrates them as four planets circling around the company's "world," and they are able to exert varying degrees of influence at different times and sets of circumstances. Each planet has its own identifying group of features under a collective designation:

- **External Environment**
- **Internal Environment**
- **Resources**
- **Energizing Influences**

If there is any final message on the subject of a culture of participation, it is that it should be an environment that people enjoy. Without enjoyment and celebration of success, people will regard work as something which detracts from their personal happiness as opposed to a means of obtaining it, and the modern expression "get a life" may just be the incentive to take their energy and expertise elsewhere.

THE ACHIEVEMENT CYCLE

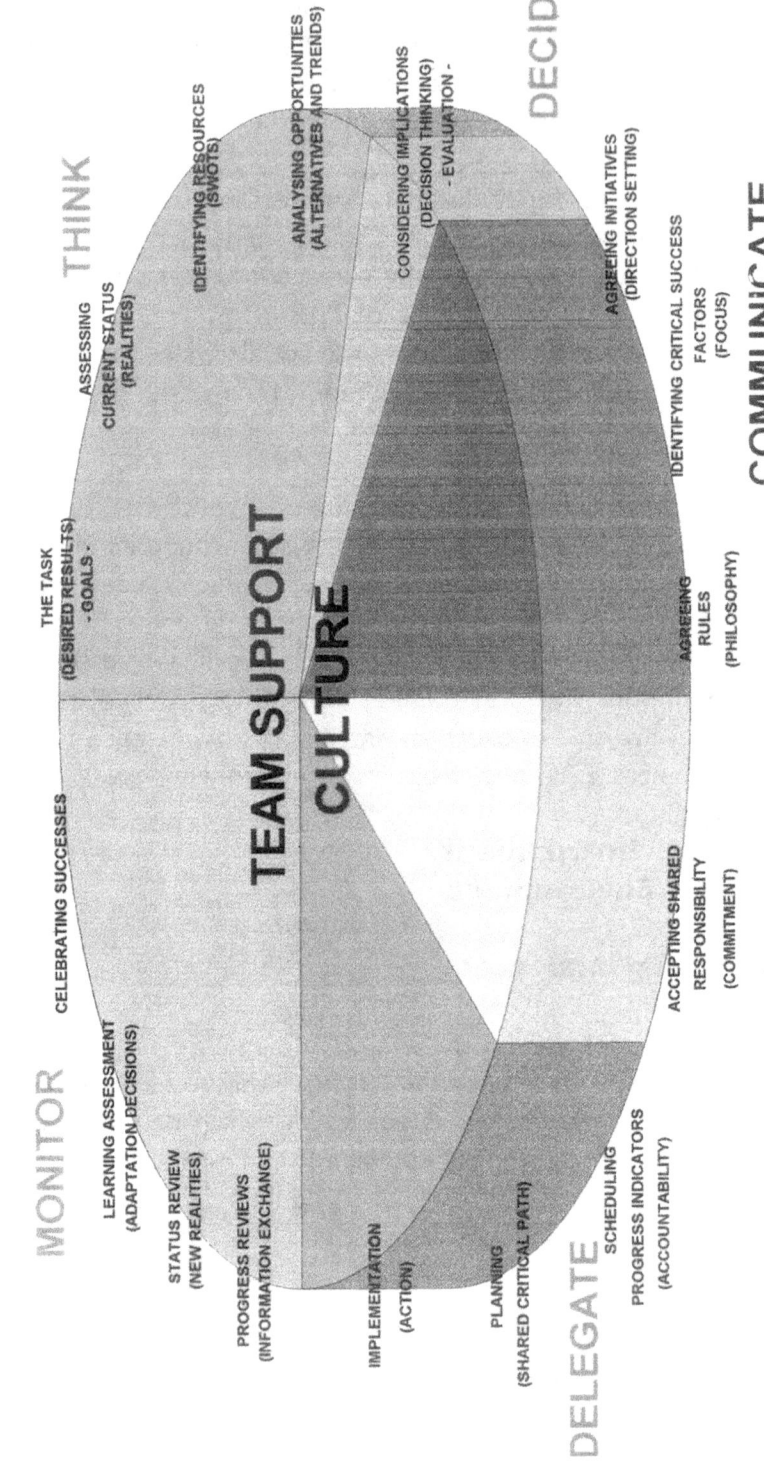

THINK
- THE TASK (DESIRED RESULTS) - GOALS -
- ASSESSING CURRENT STATUS (REALITIES)
- IDENTIFYING RESOURCES (SWOTS)
- ANALYSING OPPORTUNITIES (ALTERNATIVES AND TRENDS)

DECIDE
- CONSIDERING IMPLICATIONS (DECISION THINKING) - EVALUATION -
- AGREEING INITIATIVES (DIRECTION SETTING)

COMMUNICATE
- IDENTIFYING CRITICAL SUCCESS FACTORS (FOCUS)
- AGREEING RULES (PHILOSOPHY)
- ACCEPTING SHARED RESPONSIBILITY (COMMITMENT)

DELEGATE
- PLANNING (SHARED CRITICAL PATH)
- SCHEDULING
- PROGRESS INDICATORS (ACCOUNTABILITY)

MONITOR
- CELEBRATING SUCCESSES
- LEARNING ASSESSMENT (ADAPTATION DECISIONS)
- STATUS REVIEW (NEW REALITIES)
- PROGRESS REVIEWS (INFORMATION EXCHANGE)
- IMPLEMENTATION (ACTION)

TEAM SUPPORT

CULTURE

MODEL TWO—AMO—ELEMENTS OF IMPACT

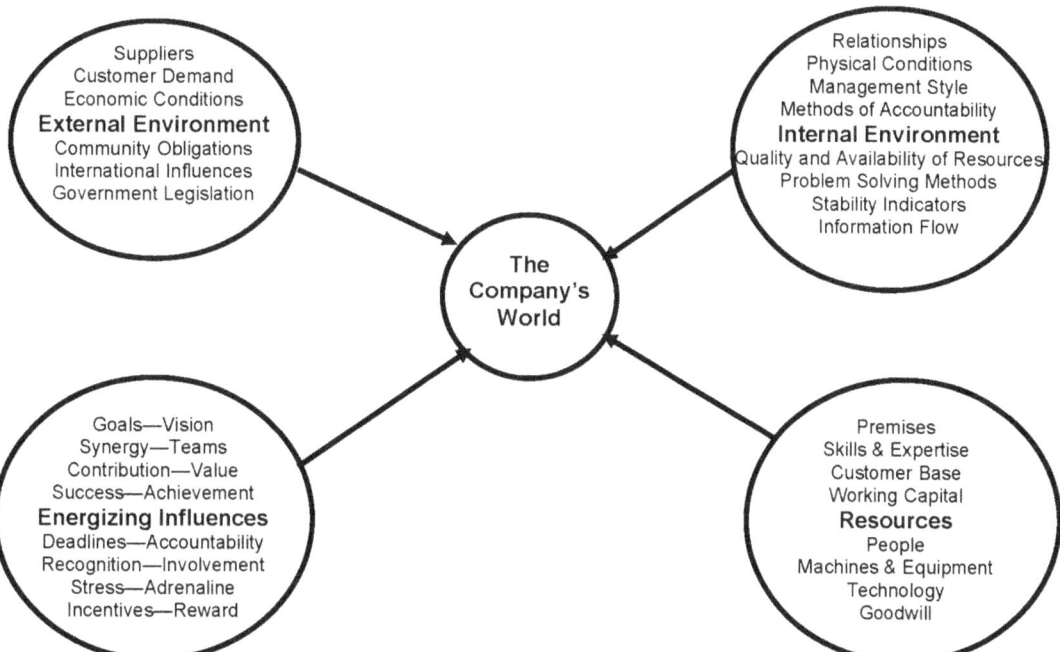

Suppliers
Customer Demand
Economic Conditions
External Environment
Community Obligations
International Influences
Government Legislation

Relationships
Physical Conditions
Management Style
Methods of Accountability
Internal Environment
Quality and Availability of Resources
Problem Solving Methods
Stability Indicators
Information Flow

The
Company's
World

Goals—Vision
Synergy—Teams
Contribution—Value
Success—Achievement
Energizing Influences
Deadlines—Accountability
Recognition—Involvement
Stress—Adrenaline
Incentives—Reward

Premises
Skills & Expertise
Customer Base
Working Capital
Resources
People
Machines & Equipment
Technology
Goodwill

CULTURE OF PARTICIPATION

CHAPTER 9

Tenet Number 9—Monitoring Elements of Impact

"No loss should hit us which can be avoided by constant care—this must be a watchword throughout the entire organisation."
(A.P. Moller in a letter to his son Maersk McKinney Moller)
With Constant Care… A.P. Moller: Shipowner 1876-1965, by Ove Hornby

If you have been involved in a car accident when you have been driving along very carefully, obeying all the rules, perfectly sober, and alone in your vehicle with no distractions, you will have learned that there are times when the unpredictable can happen and change the course of your journey, if not your life. The impact of someone else's action or decision has resulted in inconvenience or even injury to yourself. However, had you not been so conscientious and alert, the damage might have been much worse. So the fact that unpredictable and unplanned things can and do happen does not mean that we should adopt a *laissez-faire* attitude. The fact that you are normally careful to avoid mishaps probably means that most of the time you do. The same thing applies in business.

There are many things you can control, but there are others that have an enormous impact on your business but over which you have little or no control. The important thing is to be clear about all those things that in the previous chapter I have called "Elements of Impact." Some of them are related to company internal values, policies, culture, or strategic plans, whilst others are impositions from external sources that cannot be ignored or dismissed. These are usually legislative or marketplace demands. Whether they are internal or external, however, they have to be regularly observed. Like driving, maintaining alertness to trends and indicators that could have an impact reduces the likelihood of being too late to take avoiding action when something threatening or perilous confronts us.

So how do we carry out this monitoring process in a very busy and demanding business environment and ensure that it becomes part of the organizational ethos?

The starting point is to acknowledge that any enterprise exists in various states of mutual dependency with people and organizations both within and without itself. If that acknowledgement is real, the next stage is the realization that there is a need to maintain communication with these others. It is in their interest that your business stays in a healthy state and has a promising future. In other words, they are stakeholders and, as such, will want to help in the guardianship of the company's stability and strength. The task is then to put in place channels of communication that enhance the relationships between the company and its stakeholders.

How do good leaders ensure that these relationships are productive? Only by examining their personal attitudes towards them in the first place because leaders' attitudes and behaviors always have more effect on culture than all the notices, memos, and directives that proclaim how things should be done but fall into the "don't do as I do, do as I say" category.

How much respect does the leader as an individual have and display for the customers, the suppliers, the shareholders, the employees, and the community at large? Are the suggestions and concerns of these others ever truly invited for consideration and seriously listened to, or is "lip service" the reality? Is there mutual respect for each other's interests, or is there grudging tolerance and underlying distrust with no sense of loyalty on either side?

As I referred to in Chapter 6, research which stimulated the formation of The Centre for Tomorrow's Company identified that those enterprises that have withstood the test of time and maintained their stability over many years and fluctuations of fortune have been those who have placed a high value on integrity towards their stakeholders.

The Centre continues to advocate its "inclusive approach" to business operation. Inclusiveness requires investment of time and effort to ensure that company policies and practices are not carried out that exclusively benefit one set of stakeholders at the expense of the others either individually or collectively. It requires sustained commitment as opposed to the "short-termism" that is inherent in quick-profit cultures. It is not always easy to maintain, but in the final analysis, there are few ultimate advantages to be derived, with the possible exception of the gains made by a few gamblers.

Sensible organizations that are there for the long haul question themselves about the currency and accuracy of their knowledge of stakeholder attitudes towards them.

- Would the majority of their staff recommend friends or family members to work for the company?
- Would the majority of their suppliers make extra effort to maintain the quality of service they deliver because they are convinced that the company is not taking unfair advantage of them? (They are partners in a drive for ongoing success.)
- Do their customers support them in lean times and stay with them because they are convinced that their own needs are truly understood and cared about?
- Are the shareholders mainly long-term investors because they believe that the executives have the judgment, skill, and integrity to maintain the health and

good reputation of the company? (They feel assured of a reliable return on their investment to fund their own aspirations.)

- Does the community appreciate the presence of the company and trust its reputation as a body which is an asset and not a threatening liability in its midst? (Will they continue to give it a license to operate and not boycott their products or services because of perceived unethical policies and practices?)

Regular exploration of these questions by various means needs to be seen as an important priority of management who must remember that good communication is a two-way process with the emphasis on good listening. Genuine interest is at the heart of the process, and Robert Townsend's advice in his book *Up the Organisation* exhorts us, "If all else fails, try honesty!"

Dishonesty, malpractice, or the perceived taking of unfair advantages inevitably come to light one way or another, as recent events have proved. Reputations that have taken much effort and often many years to build can rapidly be seriously damaged or destroyed.

It is incredibly stupid on the part of companies to underestimate the intelligence of observers or the importance of integrity and sound judgment. The speed at which rumor, speculation, and suspicion can spread, particularly with today's technology and media organizations that greatly influence opinions, is unprecedented. Some companies are now instigating "blog" Web sites on the Internet as a means of getting instant, first-hand opinions. The message has become loud and clear to them.

Be aware of those things and people who can affect the operation of your enterprise, and constantly strive to be one of those good managers who *know what's going on*!

The following are some helpful tests you can use to monitor the state of your business:

Can you truthfully say "yes" to these acid test statements? The majority of people in our organization can:
- Explain the organization's objectives and goals
- Explain the importance of their job in relationship to the organization's success
- Demonstrate how training and development has helped them to improve their contribution to the organization
- Tell you their manager is competent and committed to coaching and developing them
- Accept responsibility to improve themselves and their job continually

Could you envisage a scenario in which the business is a living thing that you are taking to a clinic for a fitness check and having to answer the kind of questions that would lead to a diagnosis and health improvement recommendations?

BUSINESS FITNESS CHECKLIST

How is the business feeling today?

How old is it?

What are its vital statistics?

Does it have any disabilities or ailments?

Is it in pain anywhere?

Why does it feel the need for a checkup?

What is its ancestry?

How vulnerable is it to ill health?

What level of fitness would it like to attain?

How challenging a regime of habit changing will there have to be to get it there?

What culture has it been reared in?

What options are there on offer?

What advice/expertise does it need to seek?

What are its strengths?

What are its weaknesses?

What could it be doing? (opportunities include...)

What does it have to beware of?

Who/what influences its future?

Where does it expect to be in the next three to five years?

What will be the implications?

Who will be the fitness coach?

How much power/influence/credibility does the fitness coach have?

Who might be the supporters and detractors?

What are the obvious priorities?

Who will be the guide in the new journey to the future?

DIAGNOSTIC SUMMARY

SYMPTOMS CAUSING DISCOMFORT:
(Performance Indicators)

DIAGNOSIS:
(Conclusions on Level of Fitness)

PROGNOSIS:
(Predictions on Likely Progress)

HEALTH PLAN:
(Prescription and Sources of Help)

Of course, it goes without saying that one of the most significant elements of impact on a business is the state of its finances. An amazing fact is that many directors of companies do not recognize the need for them to manage the financial structure and performance of the enterprise they have created or have responsibility for. They fail to differentiate between *accountancy*, which is a historical activity, and *financial management* which is essentially an activity which has its focus on the future and is mainly concerned with **planning for profit.** The annual accounts produced by the company accountant is mainly a statutory requirement for tax purposes, and many business owners just wait for this to be presented to them for approval and signature. Their chief interest in them is to see whether or not they can see an overall profit for the last year's activities or not. Then they get back to what they see as "the day job"—that is, the important thing of running the business. What they fail to appreciate is that they should be using that report as their main source of data to be analyzed in order to find the clues to the direction the business should be taking. In other words, they should us it as a *financial management tool.*

A long-term and highly esteemed friend of mine, consultant Vivian Stokes, introduced me to this philosophy many years ago, and the first time I attended one of his workshops I was amazed at how excited I became about the use of financial data as a means of obtaining huge improvements in a business's performance by understanding how to arrive at the reality of its financial state. Where was it missing opportunities? Where was it wasting resources? Which products were the real money spinners? Which were the white elephants? Was the business starved of resources and eventually going to die of exhaustion? What was draining its lifeblood and energy? I had never believed that the balance sheet and the profit and loss account could produce so much real information if you knew just how to look behind the numbers and see the picture of a living, breathing entity. My approach to training and management development was never the same, and I am eternally grateful to my friend for his ability to take the mystique out of business finance for those of us who are "blinded by science" by accountants.

I will never claim to have Vivian's expertise or superb technique, but I have produced the following list of elements of financial management tools in business planning to highlight those things which are worth understanding if you are to become your own business analyst.

FINANCIAL MANAGEMENT

Key Elements of Financial Management Tools in Business Planning

1	The Balance Sheet
2	Source and Application of Funds
3	Gearing
4	Profit-and-Loss Account
5	Contribution Analysis
6	Break-Even Analysis
7	Control Information
8	Comparative Ratios
9	Added Value Analysis
10	Profit Planning
11	Cash Flow Forecast
12	Budget Preparation Considerations for Unit Managers

FINANCIAL STRUCTURE

The Balance Sheet

Shows (on a given date at year end):

1. Where the money came from
2. Where the money is tied up

SHAREHOLDERS' FUNDS	$,000	FIXED ASSETS	$,000
Issued Shares		Land & Buildings	
		Plant & Machinery	
Reserves		Vehicles	
		Furniture & Equipment	
		Trade Investments	
Subtotal (A)			
LOAN CAPITAL			
...% Debenture (B)			

CAPITAL EMPLOYED (A) + (B) = (C)

CURRENT LIABILITIES	$,000	CURRENT ASSETS	$,000
Creditors		Stocks	
Overdraft		Raw Materials	
Taxation		Work in Progress	
Dividends		Finished Goods	
Directors			
Subtotal (D)		Debtors	
		Cash & Investments	
Total (C) + (D)			

FINANCIAL ACCOUNTABILITY

Source and Application of Funds

This statement gives explanation of the published accounts showing: where the money came from in a year and where it went.

This statement is usually provided together with the Balance Sheet and the Profit and Loss Account.

Any increases on the left side	**= Source %**
Any decreases on the left side	**= Application %**
Any increases on the right side	**= Application %**
Any decreases on the right side	**= Source %**

When Sources and Applications are added up, the two sides should balance.

MAIN BENEFIT:

To clearly and quickly illustrate the use of working capital and the effect upon the business of executive decisions.

ASSESSING FINANCIAL RESOURCES

Gearing

This statement shows the ratio of a company's fixed interest debt to its equity capital.

Example:

	SHAREHOLDERS' FUNDS	LOAN CAPITAL	
$	$150,000	$50,000	
Ratio	3	1	About Right
$	$150,000	$150,000	
Ratio	1	1	Highly Geared
$	$150,000	$15,000	
Ratio	10	1	Low Geared

Note: If a company is in a "High Gearing" situation, it is vulnerable at periods of low volume trading—the question to be asked is: "Who owns the company, and can we keep their confidence so that they do not withdraw their support?"

FINANCIAL PERFORMANCE

The Profit and Loss Account

Year Ended 2008

		$,000	2006 (earliest)	2007	2008 (latest)
1	Sales				
2	Materials				
3	Wages				
4	Cost of Sales				
5	**Subtotal**				
6	Gross Profit (1 minus 5)				
7	Establishment X's				
8	Administration X's				
9	Sales & Distribution X's				
10	Financial X's				
11	**Subtotal**				
12	Pre-Tax Profit (6 minus 11)				
13	Tax				
14	Dividends				
15	Retained (12 minus 13 & 14)				
16	**Pre-Tax Profit**				

MONITORING ELEMENTS

MAIN BENEFIT:

To identify the trend over a three-year period:
      Profitability on an upward trend?
      Profitability on a downward trend?
      Profitability static?

FINDING THE BEST USE OF LIMITED RESOURCES

Contribution Analysis

	Total $,000	Variable Costs*	Fixed Costs**
Materials			
Operating X's			
Establishment X's			
Administration X's			
Selling & Distribution X's			
Financial X's			
Total Costs PTP			
SALES			

Variable Costs—The costs you only incur because you make the product.
** Fixed Costs—The costs you would incur whether you make the product or not.**

Example

Sales	$xxxx
Less costs allocable to products	$yyyy
= Contribution	$cccc

MAIN BENEFIT:

To identify the elements of costs which only occur in relation to the product which you sell, as opposed to those which exist irrespective of your level of sales.

To clarify the extent to which your level of sales is sufficient to cover your fixed costs or not.

AVOIDING LOSSES

Break-Even Analysis

This analysis identifies that level of sales when there is no profit and no loss, that is, the costs add up to the same as the sales.

BREAK-EVEN ANALYSIS IDENTIFIES TWO SORTS OF COSTS:

(A)   The ones that go up or down with changes in sales volume. For example, if you sell $20,000 of product in the year your material costs will have increased by, say, $10,000.

These are called DIRECT COSTS—they vary directly with volume.

(B)   The ones that do not go up or down with changes in sales volume. For example, if you sell $20,000 of product, the rent, rates, heat, light, administration costs, and so forth do not change.

These are called FIXED COSTS—they remain relatively fixed with change in sales volume.

MAIN BENEFIT:

To highlight those products or sales policies and activities that are incompatible with delivering required profitability.

To indicate critical points at which to review policy implications and make necessary management decisions for action to avoid, or minimize, potential loss.

BUSINESS PROGRESS MANAGEMENT

Control Information

This shows the data relating to what is happening in the business, which provides managers with facts in time to take corrective action if things are not working according to plan.

SHOWS:

1. Indicators of progress relating to departmental targets, objectives, and budgeting plans.

2. Monitoring data for *critical success factors* by department or operating unit.

3. Areas of the business which require action to avoid potential crisis situations.

MAIN BENEFIT:

Enables management team and others to access facts which justify changing priorities as reactions to exigencies.

BUSINESS MEASUREMENTS

Comparative Ratios

These are the measures of the achievements of a business, expressed in percentage terms, which collectively provide a comprehensive view of its financial structure and performance.

For example: <u>*Last Year*</u>   <u>*This Year*</u>   +/-%

1. **Latest sales**
2. **Latest pre-tax profit**
3. **Pre-tax profit % of sales**
4. **Capital employed**
5. **Turnover of capital employed**
6. **Return on capital employed**
7. **Current ratio assets : liabilities**
8. **Quick ratio debtors & cash : liabilities**
9. **Gearing outside money : inside money**
10. **Weeks of:**
    - **Debtors**
    - **Raw materials**
    - **Work in progress**
    - **Finished goods**
    - **Creditors**
11. **Working capital**

    Capital employed less fixed assets
12. **Contribution % of sales**
13. **Added value**
    - **Wages %**
    - **Overheads %**
    - **Pre-tax profit %**
14. **Break-even point % of sales**
15. **Number of employees**

     MONITORING ELEMENTS

16. **Sales per employee**

17. **Pre-tax profit per employee**

18. **Capital employed per employee**

MAIN BENEFIT:

Enables owners and executives of the business to clearly identify the trends in performance using objective measures for evaluating its worth in the marketplace.

ENSURING PROFITABILITY

Added Value Analysis

This helps to ensure the appropriateness of decisions on buying and pricing policies, as well as of utilization of resources.

Added value is created when the selling price of a product is such that the difference between the cost of production plus delivery of the end product and the price paid by the consumer is sufficient to cover the costs as well as contribute to the overheads and profits of the business.

MAIN BENEFIT:

To monitor the percent of wages, overheads, and pre-tax profit in relation to added value overall and indicate ways of increasing profit.

BUSINESS GROWTH STRATEGY

Profit Planning: The Key to Profit Growth

"Profit is an attitude of mind—you make up your mind what profit you intend to make, and you design your business to make it."

THINGS YOU MUST DO:

(a)	Set a demanding profit goal	(Your desired results)
(b)	Make a budget for overhead costs	(Monitor and control)
(c)	Produce a contribution plan	(Improve value added)
(d)	List areas for management action	(Changes to implement)

MAIN BENEFIT:

To provide clearly defined goals and measurable criteria for monitoring the progress of the business.

To highlight the need to manage overheads which demand regular expenditure even at times of crisis.

INCOME AND EXPENDITURE

Cash Flow Forecast

This is a means of planning and controlling the finances of the business and thereby ensuring the retention of investors' or lenders' confidence in the ability of the management to maintain the stability of the firm.

The Forecast shows:

1. Levels of income deriving from sales expectations and sales of assets over a specified period.

2. Levels of expenditure over the same specified period with resultant variations in use of overdraft facilities agreed with bankers.

3. Cumulative effect on profit or loss and indicators of potential examples of vulnerability to unexpected demands or downturns in sales.

MAIN BENEFIT:

One of the most useful aids to realistic appraisal of health and prospects of the business over a relatively short period of time.

An example of management's understanding of the need to ensure control of debtors' adherence to agreed terms, as well as their scheduling of any capital expenditure on fixed assets.

BUDGET PREPARATION CONSIDERATIONS

EXERCISE:

Operational unit budgets are part of the overall business performance planning activity. If an organization is consistently failing to make profit and is therefore not funding its existence, in reality it is not a business. It could more correctly be described as an "institution" or a philanthropic indulgence (or even a tax avoidance facility) on the part of the investors. As business loans most often come from the banking fraternity, neither of these two definitions is likely to apply for very long! Use the following as a checklist to start your own preparation.

Unit Manager's Considerations

CONTRIBUTION IMPLICATIONS

- Year ahead company desired financial results $
- Contribution required from operational unit $

UNIT ELEMENTS OF COST

- Personnel
- Premises (rent/council tax/service charges)
- Utilities
- Operating expenses
- Insurance
- Equipment leases/rentals
- Maintenance
- Advertising
- Promotional activities
- Vehicles
- Additional (depreciation, unplanned expenditure/contingencies)

UNIT SALES PERFORMANCE

- Department 1
- Department 2
- Department 3

- % Sales increase necessary   %
- % Cost reduction to maintain profitability   %
- Actions needed to implement any changes:
- Change implications:

MONITORING ELEMENTS

CHAPTER 10

Tenet Number 10—Continuous Learning Environment

"Learning is experience understood in tranquility."

William Wordsworth

In order to appreciate the importance of continuous learning in organizations with aspirations for growth, we need to consider two very significant questions:

- If companies have achieved a degree of success and are already employing well-qualified people, why should they need to keep learning?
- What is the nature of learning, and how is it acquired in a working environment?

To answer the first question, we only have to acknowledge the three "**Big C**" elements of impact on businesses:

- **C**hange and the incredible demands that it generates from society
- **C**ompetition from those who are determined to meet and satisfy society's demands
- **C**ustomers whose loyalty we need to maintain if we are to protect and maintain our presence in the marketplace

The "change" element and its significance is well summarized by Bob and Sally Garratt in their book *The Learning Organisation* in which they comment, "For any organisation to survive, the rate of learning has to be equal to, or greater than, the rate of change in its environment." It is worth noting that they use the word "survive" and not "grow." So we are talking here about staying in business at all!

So what does this mean to those of us who are willing to accept this summary and decide to heed its warning? Part of the answer to this is to remember the earlier definition of the "good manager"—that person who keeps awareness of what is going on, especially with the other two **"Big C"** elements. What is the *competition* up to, and what are the trends in our *customer* responses to us and our products? So we need to keep monitoring those indicators that point us to things we must *change* in order to keep up and hence, what new knowledge we need to acquire in order to implement those changes successfully.

This takes us back to the second question posed at the beginning. The question in relation to the nature of learning and how it is acquired in the working environment is one which is mainly concerned with perceptions about where and how learning is generally acquired.

Many people believe that learning only takes place in educational or training establishments and that when qualifications are obtained, the learning process, from a job perspective, has been completed. Some necessary knowledge has been gained, and skills have been demonstrated sufficiently to meet the laid-down criteria for academic or vocational competence, so it's now "on with the job, thank you and good-bye." What these people fail to realize and understand is that learning is an active and ongoing process that is taking place with every experience that we undergo throughout our lives, but because we tend to associate learning with formal situations and academia, we do not consciously accept that learning is taking place when we experience new things or solve new problems. (I will always remember what an experienced driver told me after I had passed my driving test: "Well done, you have passed your test; now you can start learning to drive.")

When the training fraternity began to realize that busy managers were quickly "turned off" in training courses but responded well to the approach described by the father of action-learning, Reg Revans, they decided that it was necessary to explore how learning actually takes place within individuals. It later became generally accepted that a most highly credible description of the learning process was hypothesized by Professor David Kolb whose model became known as the KOLB Learning Cycle. Kolb suggested that all learning is a cyclical process and that there are four stages, the first being what he described as "*Concrete Experiences.*" In other words, learning starts with an experience of something or some kind, and then we go through a period of "*Reflecting*" (second stage) on the experience and what it means to us. This triggers thoughts on what new possibilities this could create—"*Conceptualizing*" (third stage). We then consider the "*Implications,*" or pros and cons, of each possibility (fourth stage) before deciding how we will adjust our behavior or response in future to the next similar concrete experience. The human brain is wonderful because we can go through all of this in a flash, and we are hardly aware of it, but of course the same process can also happen over a much longer period of time. Over that more prolonged period it would be a much more conscious activity, especially if the first stage, concrete experience, was very bad and we know we may have to encounter something similar again. We might then be considering how we could make it easier or better. However, at each stage of our thought process, we are gaining new insights and thereby we are learning. As a result, our behavior would almost certainly be adapted, and the outcome would be different. (See Kolb Learning Cycle illustration below.)

If we acknowledge that this happens with every individual in our organization and that the degree of learning which takes place at each stage of the cycle varies from one individual to another, we can appreciate the enormous potential for creating new knowledge that we have at our disposal. Every problem, challenge, or success experienced by someone creates an opportunity for learning if people can be encouraged to see these as such. By developing an environment in which difficulties are perceived as learning opportunities as opposed to problems, we can reduce the stressful effect which worrying produces. Worry in itself is de-energizing, and we need to put our energies into finding answers and not into fretting about not finding them! The trick is to encourage people to recognize the value of their own personal reflections on their experience of working and the benefits of expressing their ideas on possibilities for experimentation on new approaches. Some of the very best learning comes from reflecting on mistakes or things which have gone badly wrong. Unfortunately, many organizations concentrate on finding someone or something to blame when it would be more beneficial to focus on what could be learned and if the outcome could be turned to some alternative advantage. Those who have heard the story of the culture in 3M that encouraged open discussion on things which do not turn out as hoped will know that this rewarded them with their worldwide, best-selling Post-it notes that most of us use every day.

Learning from mistakes requires a degree of courage and humility which is usually scarce in the macho cultures prevalent in western organizations. Because it often involves taking risks of criticism or (God forbid!) "loss of face" or even some form of corporate "punishment," the tendency is to avoid acknowledging the truth. The same kind of reluctance to face reality about the way things are done or the things we deliver that no longer meet the needs of the market we serve frequently exists. Only when organizations are willing and able to face realities in time to make necessary changes are they truly open to new knowledge creation. I mentioned earlier that many years ago when I first read Robert Townsend's book *Up the Organisation*, I quoted a piece of advice amongst the many pearls of wisdom contained in it relating to facing difficulty. You will remember that he said, "When all else fails, try honesty." Over and over again he has been proved right. Recent examples of large corporations being found out when trying to hide the truth highlight the importance of courage and integrity and the value of a culture of acknowledging mistakes and learning from them rather than trying to hide them. Only when an organization is willing and able to do this are they truly open to the new knowledge creation that emanates from the sharing that takes place amongst good teams. In very productive teams, the level of mutual trust is high. This is unlikely to be the case in an organization without integrity. Absence of a sense of corporate integrity generates feelings of unpredictability, insecurity, and hesitancy. These are not conducive to trust or confidence building. Without that confidence there will be less co-operation and so less sharing.

It is also worth noting that active involvement in something actually registers more deeply in our consciousness than being told or reading about it. This is even truer if the experience is challenging or enjoyable, and that is the reason action-learning is more attractive to both trainers and participants in learning events. Additionally, it has been found that if human beings are relaxed their capacity for learning is greater. When being playful, creativity tends to be higher. In problem-solving groups, therefore, we should not be afraid of making it fun. The payoff will most likely be higher than if the group is very serious and tense. The sharing of knowledge and enjoyment of the process reduces interpersonal and interdepartmental suspicion and mistrust. This in turn reduces the levels of anxiety and insecurity that are two of the most potent barriers to learning.

When barriers between departments and colleagues are brought down, people are able to see new horizons for both their organizations and themselves as individuals. This helps to strengthen common values and aspirations. When problem solving together, they are more likely to appreciate other people's viewpoints and difficulties and work towards common goals. It follows then that when an organization is able to create an environment of trust, where colleagues feel able to share their feelings as well as their thoughts, they are well on the way to achieving one that is conducive to learning. A willingness to exchange ideas, ask questions without fear of ridicule, take time to experiment, and to celebrate success, especially that of colleagues, are all ingredients for winning the game of survival. These things will not happen though without good leadership, and the best leaders gain respect for the actions and decisions which demonstrate their integrity and consistency. It is they who are the ones who create continuous learning environments by being part of that themselves.

I have had personal experience of helping in such an organization with such a leader. Alan Smith, who was at that time the chief executive of Anglian Water Company, one of the most respected utilities in the UK, having attended an MBA program, decided that absolutely everyone in his organization should have an opportunity to take part in learning activities. There was a need to change the culture, and a close associate of mine was instrumental in designing a program that was called "The Journey." Everyone was invited to take part in a series of developmental action-learning groups consisting of participants from a variety of departments. They had to devise projects arrived at by consensus and work on them over a significant period of time, fitting their activities around their work responsibilities and working out how to resource their projects. The response was amazing in terms of morale, energy, commitment, and self-discovery. The many who took part in it, including those of us who were facilitators of the groups, regarded it as a memorable and life-enhancing experience. It was no coincidence that Alan was steadfast in his commitment and presence, especially when evaluation of the program was periodically taking place. It reminded me of another of Townsend's quotes: "Every success I've ever had came about because I was trying to help other people... Every promotion I got...came about when I was up to my ears helping my associates to be as effective as possible." This attitude is not far removed from the concept of the servant-leader Philip Sadler refers to in his book *Building Tomorrow's Company* in which he describes its origin in the works of Robert Greenleaf in 1970.

There is no doubt that if a leader displays a willingness to learn, then others will not be afraid to admit that they, too, can learn, especially from each other. This means that when it comes to activities like new product research and development or finding new ways of approaching the marketplace, people are more inclined to listen to the ideas and suggestions of others rather than to stay entrenched in their own opinions and experience. My own philosophy is that I will never live long enough to learn all that I would like to and am not too proud to ask questions if I do not know the answers, no matter how obvious they may be to others. The skill of active listening is a key part of learning. Whilst you are talking you are not learning, but whilst you are listening you may be!

In organizations of any size, finding time to listen and truly understand what others are trying to communicate can be difficult when there are lots of distractions and the many activities of a busy workplace. That is why a major contribution to organizational learning can be an effective appraisal system. By acknowledging that it is important to periodically set aside some time to explore together the progress and challenges of the role that an individual has to perform, managers can often discover the causes and remedies of blocks to productivity. Unfortunately, too many managers still perceive the purpose of appraisal is to pass judgment on others and their performance. When this happens, it is invariably a wholly unproductive activity because it triggers anxiety, defensiveness, de-motivation, and sometimes even resentment. Responses are more likely to be positive when the focus of the discussion is on the future and not on the past. By inviting people to discuss their thoughts on how things are going and how "we" can keep improving, colleagues will feel less threatened, and having had an input into the planning for improvements will be more likely to be committed to whatever action is necessary to make it happen. So the more "active listening" there is on the part of the manger, the more productive the outcome.

I often relate an example of the truth of this that took place in my early days as a training adviser within the UK government's Distributive Industry Training Board. It was my responsibility to encourage companies to implement systems of appraisal as a means of improving their approach to training and so avoid paying a statutory levy to their industrial training board. I suggested to the proprietor of a small wholesale distribution company that he might try having one-to-one discussions with his staff at least annually, with the objective of improving performance all round. He felt that this approach was only applicable to large organizations but finally agreed to give it a try. We decided that if he did not judge it to be beneficial, then his opinion on its suitability for his small organization would be justified. When I returned some weeks later to receive his views on the benefit or otherwise, he told me that he would not

CONTINUOUS LEARNING

be doing this once a year, he would be doing it every month. Three of his drivers had come to see him after he had carried out the exercise and told him that they had been discussing it and wanted to make a suggestion that they should come in to work half an hour earlier in the morning so that they could get started on their rounds before the traffic rush hour. This meant that they could also then avoid the evening traffic congestion, be back at their base earlier, and be better able to prepare for the next day. The proprietor commented to me that if he had suggested to them that he would like them to come in earlier in the morning, there would have been (to use his words) "all hell let loose." The point is that it was their idea, and they responded to the fact that they had been invited to make suggestions and had been listened to.

Some readers may be curious about what is meant by active listening. The difference between just hearing and active listening is that in the latter case the listener is careful to try to understand what exactly the speaker is trying to convey and is prepared to check for mutual understanding where any doubt exists. They may ask, "Do you mean that…?" and when the answer is yes they will know that they have properly understood, but when it is no or not quite they can ask for further explanation. In Chapter 3, I mentioned the poster illustrating the likelihood of misunderstandings in communication, and misunderstandings are the supreme examples of the causes of blocks to productivity, teamwork, and learning. By taking short periods of time out occasionally to renew our joint commitment to progress, we are making a considerable contribution to ongoing success. Appraisal systems need not be overly formal or overloaded with paper and form-filling. What is important is the two-way element of the process. It should be a discussion, not a lecture on the part of the manager! This potentially highly rewarding activity has frequently been blighted by unskilled managers failing to understand the importance of empathy in interviews of this nature. This has resulted in resistance, often on the part of both managers and those whom they should be motivating. Instead of being perceived as a source of guidance, they place themselves in the role of critical judge whose main objective is to make their team members feel threatened and dominated. The prospect of arousing defensive conflict then often results in avoidance or perfunctory lip service to an activity that, in my opinion, is the foundation of good management, and everyone loses.

To summarize the formula for the creation of a continuous learning environment, we should:
- Acknowledge the value of the collective experience within the organization no matter how large or how small.
- Recognize that all learning derives from experiences followed by the productive cycle of the thought process that results in new insights.
- Encourage the sharing of insights by abolishing a culture of blame that may exist following mishaps.
- See mistakes as opportunities for learning that can be used to prevent any repetition.

- Create opportunities for collective problem solving and the sharing of lessons learned from previous mistakes.
- Never assume that only the leaders have the wit to see what's wrong and how improvements can be made.
- Set aside time for effective exploration of individual, departmental, or organizational progress and for making improvement plans or the setting up of project teams.
- Celebrate successes and always show respect for the contribution that individuals at all levels of the organization make to the "Ideas Pool."
- Be prepared to have the word "learning" in everyday parlance throughout the organization so that it becomes a recognized priority.
- Make sure that the leadership element exists in and is apparent in learning events and activities so that people can trust in its reality and that it is not just a gimmick to be ignored when the going gets tough.

LEARNING

"Teachers open the door, but you must enter by yourself."

It has been said that, on average,

WE REMEMBER

20% of what we read
30% of what we hear
40% of what we see
50% of what we say
60% of what we do

AND

90% OF WHAT WE SEE, HEAR, SAY, AND DO!

KOLB LEARNING CYCLE

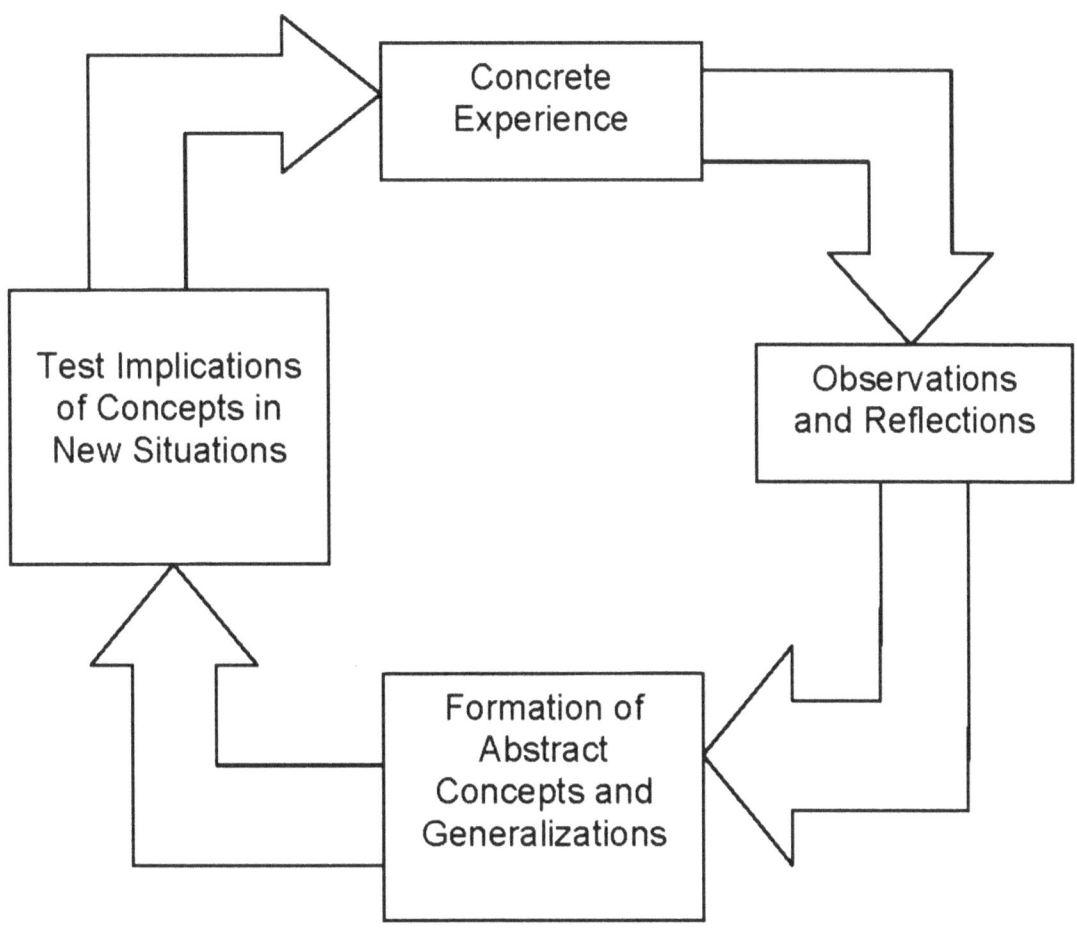

TO BE EFFECTIVE, THE LEARNER NEEDS FOUR ABILITIES

He or she must be able to:

1. Involve him or herself fully, openly, and without bias in a new experience (CE)
2. Reflect on and observe these experiences from many perspectives (OR)
3. Create concepts that integrate his or her observations into logically sound theories (AC)
4. Use these theories to make decisions and solve problems (TI)

CHAPTER 11

Summary—The Preeminent Role of Thinking in Entrepreneurship

Since this book is mainly aimed at entrepreneurs who want to grow their businesses, it is appropriate that, in the final analysis, we should consider what makes the difference between the average manager and the entrepreneur. There is no doubt in my mind that it is the extent to which the entrepreneur uses right-brained thinking.

It is my firm conviction that managers are paid to think, whether or not they realize or acknowledge that fact. It is also true that much of management requires a high degree of administration which is mainly a left-brained activity and is frequently of the kind that entrepreneurs tend to hate or at least avoid.

Currently there is some research taking place to try to find out if there is an "entrepreneur gene" that the high-profile and successful leaders of businesses are blessed with but which is not necessarily present in others. I shall be most interested in the result.

Consider three noticeable qualities in these remarkable people that indicate an intuitive ability to greatly influence the attitudes and responses in others. These are charisma, empathy, and curiosity, qualities that are often apparent in great leaders in other fields. It is my contention that these are not things that can be taught, but they can be enhanced, given the right environment.

The fact that curiosity is one of them leads me to suggest that this is the reason for the low boredom threshold so often evident in their behavior and attitude to work and education. There is no doubt that the entrepreneurial mind is happiest and most productive when it is exploring possibilities, asking "what if," and demanding variety. Sticking to routines and being constrained by habitual tasks will induce irritation and withdrawal by them from group endeavor.

Reg Revans comments that, "learning is about recognising not what we know but what we don't know," and this is why businesses must nurture those with the entrepreneurial thinking style. The right-brained exploring minds will be the ones that will keep coming up with the ideas which will take us down new pathways to the future. The powerful and high-speed activity of the right brain when engaged in imagination is awesome, so why disregard or underestimate such an asset?

Ross Perot is reputed for his "intuition" and Richard Branson for his "sixth sense." What they both display is the apparently uncanny ability to sense the future because their brains are subconsciously linking together disparate pieces of stored information and observations. Without conscious effort, rather like Einstein's imagining of climbing up a sunbeam which led to him forming his theory of relativity, they will experience resulting moments of inspiration or significant insights when they just **"know"** that something is a distinct likelihood, but cannot yet prove it. The amazing thing is that they are so often later proved right.

Perot said, "Most new jobs won't come from our biggest employers. They will come from our smallest. We've got to do everything we can to make entrepreneurial dreams a reality." He was absolutely right, and we should all share his optimism rather than using up energy worrying about the loss of jobs created by the many large organizational shifts of operations to countries who are desperately working at bringing their economies and their people out of dire poverty. We have the choice of changing places with them and becoming the losers, or we can harness the magic of our creativity and believe his other comment: "You don't have to be the biggest to beat the biggest."

Richard Branson displays all the indicators of the entrepreneurial personality. Like Perot, he started his great variety of business activities at an early age. He epitomizes the fun-loving risk taker who is willing to "have a go," and he encourages others to go with him. He has said, "It is important for the company's sake that the chairman does not get bored," and he pays little attention to his critics. He is too busy being interested in learning new things. Learning and having fun are both enormously energizing for all involved, and Branson realizes this. In a conversation, he once said, "I always have tried to make sure I work from an environment that's pleasant and fun. If the chairman's having fun, it's easier for everyone else. And if it's fun, you're going to keep going until you drop."

An old adage says "curiosity killed the cat," but another is that cats have nine lives, so they can afford to take risks. Let's face it; they always land on their feet when they jump!! So, long live curiosity. An inquiring mind is a lively mind, and lively minds are less likely to shrivel and atrophy.

Of course, once a small business starts to grow, we need the managers with their MBA-type thinking. Masters of Business Administration have been educated to concern themselves with strategy, plans, systems, pragmatism, short-term results that can be measured, and the realities of day-to-day operations. Our entrepreneurs, however, soon become bored with the activities necessary to plan and set up the systems to operate the organizations that grow from each "new baby" that they bring to life. But we must never allow the pragmatists to stultify the thinking and creativity of all employees. Atrophy comes from lack of nourishment, and an organization that crushes attempts at experimentation will eventually starve people of motivation and energy.

Maintaining the balance between creativity and focus on results is the task of the leader, who needs to recognize how to use the strengths of both to best advantage. Well-facilitated action-learning groups are the ideal vehicle for building a culture of teamwork based on mutual respect.

In earlier chapters, I referred to the value of the professional decision thinkers leading a group of decision thinkers, the benefits of sharing knowledge as a means of discovering new knowledge, and the joint monitoring of critical success factors as a contribution to optimum risk management as well as being the indicator of any need to adapt.

All of these can be achieved by the cultivation of whole-brain thinking within the management team. Each of us has our preferred thinking style, and every style has its strengths and limitations. But by acknowledging the strengths, maintaining the awareness of the limitations, and facing the challenges together as "comrades in adversity" (to borrow another descriptive phrase from Reg Revans), we can win the prizes in the competition for business success in tomorrow's world.

If this little book has set you thinking and led you to explore new possibilities, created a desire in you to learn more, or pointed you in a different direction, then I have fulfilled my task. Have a fantastic future.

In 1985, Konosuke Matsushita said in a lecture to the RSA (The Royal Society for the encouragement of Arts, Manufactures, and Commerce):

- We are going to win, and the industrial West is going to lose. There is nothing you can do about it, because the reasons for your failure are within yourselves. For you, the essence of management is getting the ideas out of the heads of the bosses into the hands of labor.
- For us, the art of management is the art of mobilizing and pulling together the intellectual resources of all employees in the service of the firm....Only by drawing on the combined brain power of all its employees can a firm face up to the turbulence and constraints of today's environment.

WAIDHA?

(WHAT AM I DOING HERE ANYWAY?)

AN EXERCISE IN THREE PARTS:

- **ME AND MY JOB**

- **CHANGE—THE COMPANY AND ME**

- **THE FUTURE—THE COMPANY AND ME**

GUIDELINES FOR COMPLETION OF WAIDHA

"WHAT AM I DOING HERE ANYWAY?"

This document has been designed to assist you to analyze your role and function within your own organization and to identify any areas in which you may feel some action or change is necessary.

It is important that you answer as factually and truthfully as you can in order that the exercise fulfills its purpose.

This is an excellent opportunity for you to examine developments within your own sphere of responsibility and to make constructive comments (addressed to yourself) leading towards some positive decisions made from a base of objectivity.

This is a private and personal analysis document which you may choose to complete as a questionnaire, or alternatively you may wish to concentrate on only certain questions which stimulate a more in-depth examination of specific areas of relevance.

Some people find the document a useful basis for discussion with colleagues to enhance the expansion of their thoughts on each topic, but others prefer to deal with the analysis on a private and quiet basis. The choice is yours. It is advisable, however, to view the WAIDHA analysis as a starting point and to refer back to it periodically to monitor your own progress.

EXERCISE: WHAT AM I DOING HERE ANYWAY?

OBJECTIVE:

To clarify your perception of your own job and how you perform in relation to the aims and policies of your organization.

BRIEFING NOTES:

All of the questions in the following pages are written in the first person and should be read and carefully considered before being fully answered.

Each question has been allocated at least one half page, but if you feel that you require more space to write, please do not be constrained by this—use additional sheets.

This document has been designed as a tool for stimulating management thinking.

It can be used as a personal development workbook or as a checklist for team discussions between the manager and colleagues.

WAIDHA

PART I

ME AND MY JOB (WHERE AM I?)

1. **What is my perception of the company's trading policy?**
    (How would I describe my organization, its culture, and the way it conducts its business?)

2. **How do I perceive marketing as a business philosophy?**

3. **What is the purpose of my job in the context of the company's aims?**
(What is the organization actually paying me to achieve?)

4. **How clear am I about what is expected of me and how (upon what basis) am I judged?**

5. **Who can influence my future?**

THE PREEMINENT ROLE

6. **Do I recognize all my various areas of responsibility, and could I list them?**
(What are the things for which I am held accountable whether I do them myself or delegate them to others?)

7. **In terms of quality of performance and results, what criteria would I use to measure my own performance?**
(If I was paying my own salary to someone else to do my job, how would I decide if it was value for money?)

8. **What percentage of time do I spend on each of my areas of responsibility within the job as a whole, and what is their order of priority?**

List responsibilities and estimate approximate average percentage of time spent on each.

Things I have to deal with	% I feel it actually is (TIME)	% I feel it really ought to be

9. **What developments or problems do I think will occur in my area of responsibility over the next 6–12 months?**

(a) Internal to the company

(b) External to the company

10. **What action will I need to take to deal with these developments or problems?**

WAIDHA

PART 2

CHANGE—THE COMPANY AND ME
(WHERE AM I GOING?)

11. How would I describe the company's position in global marketplace terms?

THE PREEMINENT ROLE

12. **Irrespective of our size, do I see the company as "world-class oriented" in the way our business is conducted?**

13. **How significant is the impact of technology on the operation of:**

(a)   The organization?

(b)   My own job?

14. **How would I describe the impact of political, economic, social, and technological trends on the policies and current practices of the company?**

15. **Which of the developments identified in Questions 9–12 will have the most significant impact on how I perform my job?**

    (a)   Internal

    (b)   External

16. **What action (if any) will I need to take to deal with the more universal developments or problems which might impact upon our operation?**

(a)

(b)

17. **If I could make any kind of changes within my job as a whole which would have a beneficial effect, what would they be?**
(For example people, location, equipment, systems, practices, and so on.)

18. In which order would I rank changes to achieve the best results soonest?
(Which would have the most significant impact?)

19. What will be the likely implications of any changes?
(List)

20. What contribution would this make towards performance aspirations within the organization?

21. Will I need support to enable me to carry out this action/change, and if so from whom?

Nature of Change	Actions Required	Support Required—Whom

22.   How confident do I feel that I will be able to obtain this support?
(Why or why not?)

23.   What are the financial considerations?

24. Is there anything I feel I need to learn in order to assist me in carrying out these actions?

25. Are there any training implications for myself or others, and if so what resources are available in terms of cost, accessibility, and quality of delivery?

26. **What are the funding and/or job coverage implications?**

WAIDHA

PART 3

THE FUTURE—THE COMPANY AND ME
(HOW DO I GET THERE?)

27. Where do I feel the greatest potential exists for improving my contribution to the organization?

28. **As a result of the previous question, what are my main SMART objectives over the next 12 months?**
(Things to be achieved within a specific time which will be seen to be contributing to a better performance overall.)

29. **What can I do to ensure that I achieve these objectives?**

30. **Have I considered ALL that I can do to achieve these objectives?**
(That is, have I considered what I delegate, internal communications, working relationships, use of all available resources, and so forth?)

31. **What results/consequences will the achievement of any of my objectives have on the company?**
(That is, in terms of finance, manpower, stress, working environment, and so on.)

32. **How convinced am I that I am (or will be) doing the right things, in the right way, for the right reasons, and at the right times?**
   OR—WHAT ON EARTH AM I DOING HERE ANYWAY?

THE PREEMINENT ROLE

MY NEW BEGINNING—A PERSONAL CONTRACT

THOSE THINGS I WILL:

STOP	
START	
CHANGE	
CONTINUE	
DO MORE OF	
DO LESS OF	
DELEGATE	
APPRECIATE	
Signed	
Date	

MY WAY FORWARD

My Goals	
My Aims	
My Objectives	

FURTHER READING

Building Tomorrow's Company
Philip Sadler
Published by Kogan Page Limited   ISBN 0-7494-3710-3

Effective Marketing
Geoffrey Randall
Published by Routledge   ISBN 0-415-10236-7

Emotional Intelligence
Daniel Goleman
Published by Bloomsbury Publishing Plc   ISBN 0-7475-2830-6

Further Up the Organisation
Robert Townsend
Published by Hodder and Stoughton   ISBN 0-340-37757-7

Leaders We Deserve
Alistair Mant
Published by Basil Blackwell Limited   ISBN 0-631-14321-1

Leadership Secrets of Attila the Hun
Wess Roberts
Published by Bantam Press   ISBN 0-593-01686-6

Leading from the Heart
Kay Gilley
Published by Butterworth-Heinemann   ISBN 0-7506-9835-7

Living Tomorrow's Company
Mark Goyder
Published by Gower Publishing Limited   ISBN 0-566-08020-6

Mary Parker Follett, Prophet of Management
Edited by Pauline Graham
Published by Harvard Business School Press ISBN 0-87584-563-0(hc)
            ISBN 0-87584-736-6(pbk)

Mind Your Manners
John Mole
Published by Nicholas Brealey Publishing   ISBN 1-85788-085-4

Productive Workplaces
Marvin R. Weisbord
Published by Jossey-Bass Publishers   ISBN 1-55542-054-0

Superboss
David Freemantle
Published by Gower Publishing Company Limited   ISBN 0-566-02588-4

Thriving on Chaos
Tom Peters
Published by Macmillan London Limited   (Book Club Association)

What They Don't Teach You at Harvard Business School
Mark H. McCormack
Published by William Collins Sons & Company Limited   (Book Club Association)

With Constant Care... A.P. Moller: Shipowner 1876-1965
Ove Hornby
Published by J.H. Schultz Information,   ISBN 87-569-2358-9

The 4%
Dr. Gerald Kushel
Published by Sidgwick & Jackson Limited   ISBN 0-283-99174-7

The Games People Play
Eric Berne
Published by Penguin Books   ISBN 0-1200-2768-8

The Grand Strategist
Mike Davidson
Published by Macmillan London Limited   ISBN 0-333-63651-1

The Learning Organisation
Bob Garratt
Published by Gower Publishing Company Limited   ISBN 0-566-02743-7

The Professional Decision Thinker
Ben Heirs
Published by Sidgwick & Jackson Limited   ISBN 0-283-99394-4

The Seven Cultures of Capitalism
Charles Hampden Turner and Alfons Trompenaars
Published by Doubleday

ISBN 0-385-42101-X

The Winning Streak Workout Book
Walter Goldsmith and David Clutterbuck
Published by George Weidenfeld & Nicolson Limited

ISBN 0-297-78704-7

FURTHER READING